Raw Tears

Yusuf Ali El
Joe H. Mitchell

NATURAL RESOURCES UNLIMITED

Hammond, IN

Natural Resources Unlimited, Hammond, IN 46320

Edited by Diane Flowers-Martin

Printed by United Graphics Inc.
Printed in the United States of America
First Printing

ISBN 978-0-912475-00-4
Library of Congress Catalog Control Number 2011916659

Cover and interior book layout and design by Borel Graphics
Cover Photography by Farrad Ali

**A Special Dedication to a
Very Special Man,
To My Father,
FRANK LEE MITCHELL**

You taught me to dream.
Mom was practical. You were the dreamer.
Mom was the realist. You were the visionary.
You were the "bread winner."
She was the "bread stretcher."
Thanks, to the two of you,
I am a practical dreamer, but with a little bit
more of you in me than of her.
Thank you "Big Frank" for teaching me
to dream beyond my means.
Your favorite son,
Yusuf & Joe

DEDICATION

To my wife-to-be, whomever she may be
& to a few people who are closer than "Six Degrees of Separation." Here goes the **"RAW TEARS TOUR"** roll call:
To my children: Gregory, Quenna, Yusuf-the-2nd, Yeshua, & Nehemiah, **my** grandchildren: Julianne and Gregory Gillenwater, my great-grandson, Kemonte, **my** brothers: Frank and Tom Mitchell, to: Doris Harris Gayles, Ann Bassett, Jamaal Gayles, Dr. Beverly Normand, Dale Godfrey, Margie Hollins, Queen Sutton, Burl "Buffalo" Webster, Namon Arnold, Jaaika Lindo, Shaun Holt, Amasiah Lindo, Tamara LaVille, Nia Benyamin, Ann Beard, Eileen Woods, June DeLia, Denise Snyder, Cheryl Thompson, Dr. Daoud Pemberton, David Keitt, Dazalee Coffey, Betty Howery, Mother Edyth Tillman, Carmelo "CJ," Sarah Mack, Yolanda Hall, Rhoda Thompson, Andre Wells, Twanna Bonner-Bey, Deborah Highley, Harriet Varnado, Dr. Rene Bergeron, Dorothy Bogan, Andrea Olowosuko, Juel Bey, Terrence El, Dante, Tamika Murphy, Gypsi Fari, Mrs. Marilyn Miller, John W. Howard, Dawn Brooks, Sam Wright, Attorney Tasha Moore, Sonnie Finley, A.K.Y. Emmanuel El, Tiscur, Joann Porter, Ayo Maat, Clara Jefferson, Ginger Mance, Dr. Cuz, Paloma Webster, Minister

Marion Jones, Trestine Duncan, **Family Elders: (John Cox, Louis Mitchell, Patience "Sallie" Reynolds, Carol Mann)**, Robin Ellen, Akile, Sandra Graniczny, Carmelina W., Alexis & Rashad Carmichael, Rashada Dawan, Trisha Mann, DeJean Baker, Greg Buckles, Carol Clarett, Azalee "Auntie" Williams, Velvet White, Paula Goshà, Marcia Alexander, Olive DuPree, Smitty-The-Firefighter, Carlo & Mari Ruiz, Gwen Martin, Joy Washington, Beverly Ray, Carol Bradshaw, Denise Borel Billups, Diane Martin, Yolanda Jordan, Kenya English, Stella & John Williams, Sis. Jean Lynn, Princess Andrea Reddix, Toya Watson, Tanya Stanford, Kesha Carthen, Maxine & Tony, Beverly Mack-Martin, Sharee Washington, Sister Suluki, Bro. Pitts, Joseph Konya, Bro. Yemi, Carmen Brewer, Ms. Dot, The Moors: Els, & Beys, Roman & Maria Villarreal, Siera Jordan, Lise & Wendy Wilson, Donovan McClean, Sarah and Nasim Hussain, Stephanie Wilson, Kirk Dyson, DeShola, Linda English, Patsy Harris, Rhonda Hunter Simon, Kimberly Henderson, Nate Carter, Stan and Robin Henderson, Pembroke, IL., and of course, you & you.

TABLE OF CONTENTS

Table of Contents

TABLE OF CONTENTS

Table of Contents

INTRODUCTION

I want to provide a little background information in the event you wonder why I named this letter, **Raw Tears.**

Let me explain. On September 19, 2003, the words **Raw Tears**, entered my consciousness. I did not know what to do with them. I looked around my mind but could find no poem attachment — No mental images, not a single sentence accompanied their arrival. I had not even half of a clue as to the reason for their being. I had no charade of a hint as to what I was supposed to do with them. **Raw Tears**, I wrapped them in one of the usual scraps of available paper which served as receiving blankets for newborn poem thoughts.

There they were...one enigmatic pair of words, **Raw Tears**, no mother, no father, abandoned, orphaned at birth, left naked on the doorsteps of my mind. Yet, the words held such lofty promise, **Raw Tears**. They could be Moorish Royalty. They could be the new *"Open Sesame"* or simply a secret something sent to resuscitate my mind. Oh, but such promise. Yet, I had no idea what that promise was. I was intrigued. I was smitten by this mysterious phrase I had never heard or seen around town. **Raw Tears**. Who are you? What do you mean? What do you want? What am I suppose to do with you? That night, or rather in the early a.m. hours of September 20, 2003, the meaning of **Raw Tears** crept into my bed, snuggled up against me like a wet dream. I was in one of those sleep places, where not only are you aware that you are sleeping and dreaming, but you are aware of how good it feels. That's where I was. I was excited that the riddle of **Raw Tears** was solved, but I was sleeping good and did not wish to fully awaken, not even for **Raw Tears**.

I decided I would have the best of both worlds. I would recite the "dream verse" over and over in my sleep. That way, I could remember it when I woke up. It was a win-win situation. I could save the poem and hold on to the best rest I'd had in weeks.

Well, that's when I knew I had lost my mind during the night. For weeks, maybe months, I had been longing, yearning, pining to write the kind of poetry which makes me jealous of myself. I had been moping and hoping, complaining like the Brothers in the Book of Numbers, about the fish, cucumbers, melons, leeks, onions, and garlic they used to enjoy back in Egypt. And here it was, everything I had been missing, and I was too trifling to wake my lazy ass up and write it down. I cussed myself awake, took the ever present pen and paper (probably an old envelope) from my nightstand, which was probably a folding chair, and I wrote:

> *"Raw Tears————Sept.19-20, 2003.*
> *Something come to me, last night while I slept*
> *Don't-cha know God cried, where it say, "Jesus wept"*
> *I was crying Raw Tears, say my pillow's soaking wet*
> *I calls 'em Raw Tears, cause they ain't done yet."*

Raw Tears is a one-man anthology of poems, stories, and letters. Composing and compiling **Raw Tears** have been the most fun I've had in years, and also the most work. The poems go from 1969 to 2011. "Happy-Sad Blues" comes from 1969. "The Hooker" was written in 1970. "A Tribute to Annie Lee" was born October 3, 2011 and "Virtual Love Song," as recently as October 12, 2011 and just like the poem, **Raw Tears,** "I ain't done yet!"

ACKNOWLEDGEMENTS

I am deeply indebted to my Spiritual Sister, Doris Harris-Gayles, for always taking time to listen as I coaxed this book into being. Thank you for your positive input and your well argued opposition when you were not in agreement with some idea I presented. Thank you for being a wonderful sounding board and a true friend.

Thank you Doris Harris-Gayles for your unfailing friendship, and support. You are the perfect friend; you let me be me. Thank you, Yolanda Hall of Gary, IN., for your computer genius, friendship and limitless patience. I thank a new friend, Diane Martin, the novelist, and author of *Autumn Leaves, Fallen Angel, Never What It Seems,* etc. Thank you for reading my manuscript, making corrections, suggestions, and unselfishly sharing your expertise in the self-publishing arena. Thank you for recommending Mrs. Denise Borel Billups of Borel Graphics. Most, but not all of your suggestions were heeded. There were the times I expressed that I was traveling under "Diplomatic Immunity" of "Poetic Licensing," and like big city police, I did not have to obey the rules of the road and could run through red lights and normal punctuation at my discretion.

And a heartfelt thanks to all who allowed me to read my works to you as I sought to fine tune each poem. And, last but not least, I thank you, Bonnie Randall Mitchell, for reading and reciting poetry to us when we were children, and for *Doubleday's* "The Best Loved Poems of the American People." You bought it for us almost sixty years ago. I quickly claimed it as my own. I wrote my name inside. You did not mind. Bonnie Mitchell, you made me a poet. You gave birth to me twice, first, as your second son; next, as your first poet. Thank you, Mother. You are my favorite poem.

October 19, 2011

My Dear Friend,

I know it seems like it's taken forever for me to get back to you. I kept starting this letter, then something would happen, then I would put off writing you until the upheaval settled and I could include the details in the letter. Well, we both know how that worked out. Please forgive me. I could, at the least, have dropped a postcard in the mail to let you know I had not forgotten our friendship or that I owed you a letter or two. Mea culpa.

In your last letters,(I have them right here), you asked about my writing. Am I still at it like I used to be? Am I going to publish again? If so, when? Am I still writing short stories or just sticking with the poetry? Am I still "trying" to write songs? Did I marry? Am I fat? Did I go bald? Have I retired? Am I still in love with love?

Well, my Friend, things have quieted down for the moment, knock on wood. I have the house to myself for a few days, so let me bring you up to date. I hope this letter finds you well, answers your questions and raises several more. And please, pretty please, don't take as long to get back to me as I took to write you. Here goes:

IN THE BEGINNING

CHILDHOOD IN PEMBROKE, ILLINOIS

A field of grass
  birds flying o'erhead
   and here alone I lie
    watching the clouds
     with their many faces
    go rolling slowly by

Their changing shapes
  they come to me
   fantasies of believing eyes
    I marvel watching children
   run and tumble
     on soft cushions of the skies

The sky's roof
  of blues and whites
   earth's floor, an autumn brown
    the sun's rays
     flecks of hereafter
      come beaming gently down

But comes the time
  I must start home
   my imprint, it stays behind
    and the calm serenity
    that I just knew
     remains upon my mind

My Pembroke, Illinois

My childhood friends
have all gone home
to that place that follows life.
There were no crowds
at their farewells
no drum, no flag, no fife.

They passed unnoticed
and unknown,
these friends I held so near:
The evening dove,
the guinea fowl,
the rabbit and the deer.

These were my pals
my childhood friends,
the very best of folk.
And we were close
these woods and all
as acorns....to an oak.

WINTER TIME IN PEMBROKE, ILLINOIS

Early frost settles over me
in thin crisp layers
It etches abstracts on my living room window
It numbs me to the warmer realities
of Winter's possible intimacies
Hot buttered Rums
Lots of snuggling
Snow days...........Working from home

I remain inside
I clench my fists and prepare to curse the cold
I hum, "It's Summertime, and the living is easy"
I shiver prematurely; I make my teeth chatter on cue

I glimpse my mind grinning at me
My smile wins me over
Seduced again, what a sap
Later, I bundle up and mush my way
into the barely freezing
double digit Winter solstice air

I inhale deeply
My nostrils stick together, for the 1st time this year
and I wonder
After all the hell I've raised
have I grown too old
for snow angels?

I AM THE COUNTRY
(NATURE'S CHILD)

I am the country
I am dirt roads   pump water   out-houses
sparrow sounds   corn pone   and mama whippings
I am the country
I am waving corn leaves imitating country winds
evening shadows milky-ways   late night noises
cricket symphonies
and standing room only sunsets
that play to full houses each evening

I am the country
I am yard dogs breaking chains biting strangers
stealing chickens
and howling eerie superstitions
to half full moons
I am the country
I am y'all   yes'm   no'm
peck bushel gunnysack
two-bits   sweet-bread
down-the-road-uh-piece
hot toddies   goose grease
n' poke salad for your mess-uh-greens

and you and I
holding hands and pieces of twilight
like straws in our teeth
like straws in a country wind

I am .

CHILDHOOD
(CHICAGO RENAISSANCE-2)

Safety pins
and iron on patches
busted seams
and socks mismatching

That's what childhood means to me

Hi-water pants
brogan shoes
hand me down coat
seersucker suit

That's what childhood means to me

Two left mittens
two right boots
red flannel long johns
ain't he cute

That's what childhood means to me

homemade hair cuts
double-stitched seams
last year's clothes
but always clean

That's what childhood
Means to me

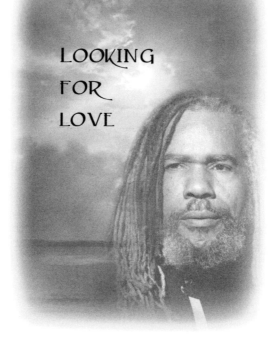

LOOKING
FOR
LOVE

HELP WANTED

Poet in the market for a good woman.

Note: We are **not** an equal opportunity employer.

Only a beautiful, talented, adventurous, sensual,

sensitive, affectionate, honest,

spiritual,

loving,

kind,

considerate,

industrious,

well-read,

educated,

down-to-earth,

drug & disease free,

positive thinking, sane,

health conscious, pork-free, confident,

unmarried, credit worthy, poetry loving woman with a
wild, warm, and wonderful sense of humor need apply

I **do** discriminate. **I am not** an equal opportunity lover
Email resume & recent photo to: yusufaliel@yahoo.com

MORE THAN A PASSIN' FANCY

To see a woman
    walking down the street
        a woman you have known
            more than just casually

    drawing all the glances
        from every guy she meets
            minding her own business
        a woman walking
            down the street

Then suddenly, you see it all
    and you cannot help recall
        how her long brown legs
        fit with yours

            when she was yours
            that year or more

And you were almost to heaven
    almost, to God's front door
        and you almost
        almost, just made it
            O you almost, knew the score

So you scheme
    and you dream
        "If she were only
        mine once more"

COURTSHIP
(REPRINTED FROM O WOMAN)

the ocean coos
like a liquid dove
come follow me
I'll show you love

the sun hovers sadly
in the western sky
like a parting lover
hating good-bye

the cool beach stretches
out her sands to me
promising peace
if I never leave

the salt wind blows
and softly woos
making me offers
I can't refuse

but I can't go
I must confess
I've promised my heart
to loneliness

INTUITION

are you in love
don't act surprised
neon's flashing
in your eyes

LOVER'S QUESTIONS

Where were you
when you first fell in love
           and knew it
at the show
at a dance
in a class
in the hallway at school

Where were you
when you said your first
           I Love You
        or I Love You Too

in someone's car
at your folk's place
      on the phone
      in front of your locker
      walking home from school

Where were you
    at the time I bet
      you never thought
      you could forget

      Where were you

THE PRE-NUP

O Woman
Each and every time we make love,
I want to make love with you,
not to you,
but with you,
for us.

No consensual rape this time,
where you submit because you're mine.

It's no climax I'm looking for,
no quickie fuck and then we snore.

No instant, open, brown, and serve,
no just add penis, then we stir.

Don't want no pussy,
don't want no snatch,

This time let's,
make love from scratch.

SIGNATURE_____

SIGNATURE_____

DATE_____

No Signature Required

When I say I love you
I do not hesitate,
for you to say you love me too,
I don't anticipate.

For loving you
is my reward,
in fact, I'm overpaid,
for yesterday, I could not love
O God, I'm glad I prayed.

I do not need my love returned
it is no lease nor loan.
It is a gift from God and me
both suitors you have known.

My love is unconditional
no ifs, no buts, no whens,
so do with it as you see fit
my love's now yours, my friend.

The Arraignment

If breaking someone's heart
were a case of B & E
the judge would throw the book at you
for what you've done to me

If stealing someone's heart
really were a crime
girl, you could be facing
a whole lot of time

We would both be old and gray
by the time they set you free
and knowing me, I'd be right there
so you could sweet talk me

O Woman (1)

If I were on the phone with God
and a call came in from you,
I would have to tell Him,
"Hey, let me get back to you;
I gotta take this."
O Woman

O Woman (2)

I love you
35 inch waist, sagging breasts,
broken veins, cellulite,
stretch marks and all.
I love you.
O Woman

O Woman (3)

when I say that I love you,
that also goes for your children too;
my mistake, I thought you knew.
If you're reading my poem
Now you do.
O Woman

O WOMAN (4)

Being near you
without touching
is like sneezing
without blinking.
Improbable,
implausible
unthinkable
impossible.

O WOMAN (5)

I love you so much
that if I were in a horrible accident
and came to, broken and bleeding
on the side of the highway,
gargling blood
and drifting in and out of consciousness,
I pray that during a lucid moment,
I would have the physical strength
and presence of mind
to dip my forefinger into my blood
and scrawl your name next to me
on the roadside before I died
As Otis Redding said,
"That's how strong my love is,"
O Woman

O WOMAN
(REPRINTED FROM O WOMAN)

O Woman,
don't feel that you
can only come to me
when things are going well.
I want you to come to me
with your tears, fears,
and clabbered promises
that sat out too many nights.

I want you to come to me
in your head rags and blue jeans,
with an old coat
thrown over your night things.
I want you to come to me
when today is gone, tonight's too long,
and tomorrow, is too far away.

I want you to come to me
when you need someone to be lonely with
and lovemaking is nowhere near your mind.
Because, you see girl, I've been lonely too,
and I know that lonely, is as chronic as cancer,
and it keeps no time schedule.
So come to me, and don't worry
about the lateness of the night.
I want you to come to me,
when it gets to you.
Just come on to me girl,
and I'll do what I can.
I'll be your friend.
O Woman.

O Woman, Just Who Are They

Just who are they to tell us
that though love can survive
it cannot grow anew
  on wrinkled hands
    and sagging faces
      slowly losing territorial disputes
        with the gravitational pull
          and eminent domain claims
            of six decades worth
              of birthdays and worry lines

              so I become the perfected spy
              the perfect safe-house
                granting asylum to tired clichés:
                hounded by a misspent youth
            wild abandon
          smoldering passions
        brooding lusts
dark desires
  white hot sex
    insatiable appetites

      who would look for them
        amid the crows feet
          and graying camouflaged plumage
            of an aged Lothario
              well practiced in the connubial arts
              Who would look for
              the legendary fountain
              of tantric erotica

here where love-making
simmers to a slow boil

steeped in patience,
sautéed to perfection
marinated
in no crass craving to climax

here, in the safety of my years
I am the fabled
trojan-wearing horse

here, I debunk myths,
establish new ones
unearth secrets
and prove to the world
that you can
teach an old dog
new tricks
watch me
fetch your heart
again
O Woman

Let Me Be Your Fool

If I could just get you to fool me
Into thinking you love me too
I'd gladly go through this life
Being a fool for you
    If you would just make sure
      That I never learn the truth
        I'd gladly go through this life
      Being a fool for you

Just pull the wool over my eyes
Make sure you keep it there
Promise me I'll never know
Of an outside love affair
    Just fool me into believing,
      That your love for me is true
        And I'd gladly go to my grave,
      Being a fool for you

If you will just promise darling
To keep me in the dark
And never let it get back to me
How you're playing with my heart
    See to it I spend my life
      Without the slightest clue
        And I'll gladly go to heaven
      Being a fool for you

MEDLEY OF LOVE

O Woman
I would rather be hurt by love,
through love, in love, with love,
than to spend another day
without you love,
as I try to make sure
that I'm never hurt again,
and in the process hurt myself
far more than any heartbreak
ever could.
I give up.
I surrender to love.
I surrender to you.
O Woman

A Quiet Love Poem

We stood still
(appropriately so)
in the middle of the street
in the middle of the night

both of us covered with snow

You, with a head full of soft flakes
and I, with a new smile breaking

and watched the absolute miracle
of God's Sunday night perfection
The December snow had come as expected
and stuck   as expected

It had performed quietly
        quickly
        magically
        turning bare birches
        into perfect Christmas ornaments

        We stood still and listened
        to the quiet night
        that was meant for sleigh bells
        and red scarves
        and hooded parkas
        and cold hands holding other hands

        And you,   And me,   And Love

TELL ME YOU LOVE ME
(CHICAGO RENAISSANCE-5)

Tell me you love me
say that you care
  lie if you have to
  but don't leave me here
I know that on high
you don't need like I need
  just because you are so strong
  don't deny me
Tell me you love me
swear it is true
  tell me you want me
  and make sure you do
Tell me you love me
speak without words
  tell me you need me
  and make sure I heard
Hold my hand often
hug me a lot
  tell me you miss me
  whether or not
Tell me you love me
say that you care
  lie if you have to
  but don't leave me here

  tell me you love me
  tell me you love me

WOMAN'S TOUCH

Like a bachelor flat
with no flowers,
no color scheme
no potted plants
no matching things

Like fine china
kitchen curtains
scented soaps and such
what my life needs
is a woman's touch

BLUES SONG FOR JIMMY REED

Was it something in the food
or something in the wine
or something in your touch
that put something on my mind
I believe, I believe
you putting yo' spell on me
duh dunt-dunt, duh dunt-dunt,
duh dunt-dunt
what got me going down baby
going down.............trying to please
duh dunt-dunt, duh dunt-dunt,
duh dunt-dunt

Was it the way you use to love me
the way you wore yo' clothes
the way you used to hug me
that opened up my nose
I believe................I believe
you putting yo' spell on me
duh dunt-dunt duh dunt dunt
duh dunt dunt
what got me going down baby
going down on my knees

got me uh homeboy superstition-girl
I do believe in sign
while you was putting out for me
you putting something on my mind
O' Yeah

Reserved Subtlety

You want that special attention
from me, when we
are on display someplace
where you don't want
some wayward female
to mistake me for available

You drink from my cup
feed me from your fork
hand me your purse
while you decide
between this silk or that leather

Subtlety scents your silent screams
He's mine! You storm
in feminine mime language
No hand on hip
no finger wagging
no neck popping
no scathing look, no obvious posturing
detectable to untrained innocent eyes

Your Alpha-female periscope 360s the room
picking up objects moving
dangerously close to your no-fly zone
Your woman-sensitive sonar
senses a stealth approach
disguised as a happily married friend
flying beneath peace time radar
triggering tramp-sensitive alerts

Bitch-in-Heat! Bitch-in-Heat!

Like a 3-time loser
in a 3-strikes and you're out jurisdiction
your hand dips into your purse
like a cornered con going for her gat
You come up with your piece
you calmly unwrap a stick of gum
discard the paper into my willing hand
You meticulously break the gum in two
You place the larger piece in my mouth
You make sure your fingers penetrate my lips
deeply enough to caress my tongue
Yeah, I love it

I love the quiet sophisticated way
you loudly stake your claim without a sound
No embarrassing scenes
but a rage visible only to the guilty
You threaten, no, you promise total annihilation
to all who will not stand down
Noiselessly, dangerously, lethally screaming
"He's mine! All mine!"
Without a word spoken
you hoist your colors over me
you adjust my collar...caress your thumb over my lips
as you remove invisible crumbs
your cool is kryptonite to my heart
like a charlatan healer, you slay me in the spirit

I love the way you mark your territory
When we are out, I accept....I am yours....then mine.
Maybe, I am hen-pecked.
But I love your cool. I just love it.

LOVE FOUND
AND LOVE LOST

BEFORE THE THUNDER
(VIGNETTES)

Our love
was not so mysterious
so embroidered with secret sign
that it could not be read
by a passing hobo
peering cautiously
from the rumbling boxcar
or by the young boy
who crossed our yard on his way
to capture tadpoles
from the algae-infested stream
Our love was a fire
a gentle caressing warmth
not a judgmental inferno
nor a giant steel mill blaze
that metal-minded men might make
It was an ordinary love
that burned in two well-seasoned hearts
and could heat two or three lives
with no trouble
It was a tender glow
that was well-banked
with the years and the triumphs
but it was enough for us
almost

♫ Virtual Love Song ♫

Let's make a date
Let's make plans
to spend the night
alone again

We'll play dress up
We'll strategize
to make our outfits
harmonize
You choose my clothes
I choose yours
something suitable
for outdoors

I'll spray the air with your perfume
to make believe you're in the room
You'll scent your space with my cologne
glance at the sky, then at your phone.
It rings, I say, "please come outside
bring your glass and raise it high."

We toast the moon
with fine champagne
I'm in Seattle
You are in Maine

Songs and poems fill the air
I'm "poeming" here; you're singing there
I run your fingers through my hair
My left hand cups your derriere

We slow dance to old Motown tunes
We toast again the waning moon.
Your scent grows faint; so does cologne
and once again we are alone

I run your fingers through my hair
My left hand cups your derriere
We slow dance to old Motown tunes
We toast last call way too soon
Your scent grows faint; so does cologne
and once again we are alone

We sip the last
of fine champagne
and just like that
we're home again

I, in Seattle
You, safe in Maine

S-E-C-R-E-T-S

white hands once touched
with ebony hands
paled lips
did softly sigh

to whisper a love
that ruled her soul
to bathe in tears
that I made cry

tonight, those nights
lie far away
but some memories
refuse to die

some nights I stray
memories scented lanes
and wonder
whose..........dark secret

am I

SEGUE TO ECSTASY:
THE RENDEZVOUS

O Woman
it was as though no time stood between us
time folded into itself; decades vanished
in the minutes it took you to get naked
you undressed like a college girl
who had never known coy
nor false modesty
I, relaxed by your ease,
ease out of my jeans
and into your arms
arms I had not worn for almost forty years
we were a perfect fit
as though a master tailor
had secretly taken our measurements
and custom cut our bodies
to one another
everything fit
lips, hips, arms, torso and timing
legs pretzeled perfectly together
eradicating all spaces between us
your body inhaled mine
slowly, slowly, ahhhhh, slowly I vanished into you
dreams do come true
and again we slowly synchronized our lives
matching each other's motions
in Room 135

SEGUE TO ECSTASY:
The Kiss

I kissed you.
I was hoping you were hoping
I would.
I did not dare ask permission.
I know me.
Any hesitation on your part
I would have taken as a "no"
even if you answered "yes."
I could not risk
having my confidence swerve.
It had taken too long
to build up the nerve
to lean down and gently dab a first kiss
against your moistened lips.
You moaned a made-for-TV-moan
that screamed a "yes"
against my mouth's caress.
You pressed up against my lips
slightly...............politely at first
then urgently,
as if you had never been kissed,
or perhaps kissed so long ago,
that it blurred and blended
with never-been-kissed at all.
Your moans, your seizure-like twisting moves
encouraged me, incited me.

Your body mimed and yes...yes...yesssed me.
Then your words,
real words this time,
Scatting yesses like Sarah Vaughn
lighting it up at the Blue Note.
Scatting yesses like a jazz diva
headlining a New York tribute to Ella Fitzgerald.

Your vowels, your consonants,
your nouns, your verbs,
your commas, your clauses,
they yessed me.
No longer just purrs and moans,
erotic incantations
awaiting translation,
but real words, unmistakable confirmations.
Yes after yes.

They swallow
any hesitation I have left.
They applaud my ears.
They massage my libido.
They play to my strengths.

and I answer with my own riffs.
and kiss! And kiss!
and kiss!

SEGUE TO ECSTASY:
PILLOW TALK

O Woman, in a single evening,
I grew accustomed to you in my arms
and I in you and in yours.
The heat of your body and Forest Street memoirs
encased & comforted me like an electric blanket
on a New Hampshire night,
when it's 12 below, & the chill factor is too-cold-to-call.
I miss you falling asleep in my arms,
and my arms, at least my left one,
going to sleep shortly after you dozed off,
with it strategically pillowed beneath your head.
I did not dare pull away and risk disturbing you.
It was one of those manly sacrifice things
that I had not experienced in way too long.
The discomfort was a badge of honor, a purple heart.
I wore it proudly that night. I flaunt it now.
I wish my fingers were still numb
if it meant you were still sleeping in my arms,
cutting off the circulation to my hand,
increasing the circulation to my heart.
A year has passed.........I yearn for the prickly
tingle of numbness as feeling slowly sneaks
back into my left hand,
as low level electric currents needle & sting my fingers
in answer to the blood flow I flex & coax back
into my painful fingertips. I am careful

not to disturb the picture perfect intimacy of you
gently snoring in my tired protective arms.
It gives new meaning to the words, "I want to sleep with you."
And I do, "I want to sleep with you."
O Woman

After All These Years and Merlot

After all these years, you are still a heady wine.
I never could hold my "lick-her" around you.
I cannot imbibe too much of you at one time.
You, I must savor, and sip. I must swish you around
in my mouth and my mouth around in you
to allow your full-bodied flavor and bouquet
to satiate my palate and intoxicate my indiscretion.
I could easily get drunk on you
and say things I mean, but don't mean to say
until you and Merlot loosen my tongue,
and cause my reservations to stagger
and collapse in a giggling heap at your feet.
I should have passed on the next to last "last call."
After all these years, how are you still the most
beautiful woman in the room? How am I still the richest man
on earth when you are on my arm?
Maybe, it's the way you say "Honey or Babe" as if
no one ever uttered those Terms of Endearment
before you. It could be the way you look at me as though I can
walk on water or "hang ten"
on a tsunami, even though you know I don't swim.
"Why am I smiling? No, why the grin?" you ask. "Are you
laughing at me?" you say, as you take a slow turn in front of a
full length mirror to see if your dress or your hair are askew.
"Just thinking of you," I reply.
"Thinking what?" you ask, with that quizzical look in your eye, as
you pat your hair. "I would know that devilish look anywhere..."

"Now tell Mama, why are you looking like the cat that just swallowed the family canary?"

"Alright, since inquiring minds want to know, when I opened your car door, I was hoping you did not do a 90 degree pivot on your perfect derriere,

and while keeping your legs closed,

place booth feet on the driveway at the same time,

then ascend to a full standing position.

You did not disappoint. I opened your door. Your right foot landed first. You knees were now a good 18-24 inches apart, as I extended my left hand in a gentlemanly fashion to assist and support. As you raised your left leg to complete your exit, your skirt rose....and so did I. As my hand guided you to your feet, I caught myself looking under your dress and liking the fact that I was liking where I was looking, after all these years. I had positioned myself so that if your southern exposure lit the evening air with the shooting stars I have seen come from there, no one but me could see."

"Now, what are you grinning at?" I ask. "Are you laughing at what I said?" "I'm laughing at us," you sighed. "For years, I have made special exits and entrances, and each one of them just for you, and I never knew if you knew, but now, I do. For the first time you have let me know that you have enjoyed the show. You make me feel like the most beautiful woman in the world. You are truly my personal, dirty old man. Is that a bag of rock candy, there in your hand?"

"O Woman, as you came downstairs, the fabric of your dress was clinging to you like the jealous husband of a much younger wife. The gentle swell of your firm behind reminded me of a seasoned smuggler sneaking forbidden booty through customs. My eyes x-rayed your body language. My gaze strip-searched you head to toe. My trained imagination completed a full cavity check, only to discover that indeed you were concealing contraband: a rare pearl tongue, pungent jewels, precious aromas, exotic fragrances, national treasures concealed between your perfumed thighs.

I'm afraid I am going to have to impound you,
when we get home this evening.
I declare, I am going to get to the bottom of this.
I am no novice at interrogation.
I have ways to make you talk and moan and scream.
Before I finish with you, you will be ready to confess
that you, and you alone "Killed Roger Rabbit."

I may have to restrain you with whip cream and silk scarves.
You may be in for a severe "tongue lashing."
I may have to water-board you with champagne
and gag you with strawberries and ripe kisses to keep your
cries of ecstasy from waking our neighbors and stirring
needless jealousies.

O Woman, you have the right **not** to remain silent during love making. By the way, have you seen the handcuffs?

TWENTY-FOUR HOURS & STILL MISSING

O woman
your faded terry cloth robe drapes
the foot of our bed, where you tossed it
that last morning you exited our bed
and my life
I have replayed the scene
thousands of times
since you went missing
I search for clues
there must be some tell-tale evidence
I overlooked..................then and now
three years cannot vanish without a trace
we made love that morning
the first time around 6 a.m.
the second time about 8:30
we loved ourselves into exhaustion
our bedroom was a sweat lodge
and Oh, did we sweat
we finally slid apart and lay on our backs
gasping for breath; laughing, accusing each other
of attempted murder
murder-suicide scream the headlines
Oh, how we laughed at that
big, loud, crazy chunks of impolite laughter
the kind that people can only laugh in places
of complete comfort and acceptance
you caught your breath and said

"I can just see the authorities
searching for suicide notes, murder weapons
and evidence of forced entry."
"Woman, you know that entry was anything but forced.
By the way, is that piece you're concealing even registered
Don't you need a CCW for what you're packing
that brought another gale of laughter
we relished the slippery ecstasy
of our most complete love-making in years
Maybe, in forever
You showered
dressed for work; had me zip you up
then kissed me deeply enough
to get us going again
you freshened up once more
"it's after 9:30. stay your distance
some of us work Saturdays," you said with a laugh
You walked out the door as you had
hundreds of times
We did not speak again that day
not until late evening when you called
to say so matter-of-factly
"I'm lost in our relationship"
"I've moved on with my life"
I have not slept in our bed
since you made off with my heart
I sleep in the chair
in what used to be our bedroom

the chair where I used to study and doze
while you were resting and I had reading to do
and just wanted to be close to you
Everything is as you left it
and yet, nothing is the same
I pray you hurry up and find yourself
because although, I am right here
I am lost without you
O Woman

LOVIN' YOU
(LOVIN' YOU)

I made mistakes
I still owe dues
 I fell down, got up
 and kept right on
 Lovin' you

I sowed some oats
in pastures wild
 stayed around
 to help them grow
 for awhile
 and kept right on
 Lovin' you

I thought about
travelling alone
 I went away
 and came back home
 and kept right on
 Lovin' you

In the morning I may leave
find a place that pleases me
 with a girl who home-makes bread
 and patchworks quilts for my bed
 And keep right on

 Lovin' you

LOVIN' YOU 2

I may go
many miles away
 I may return
 or I may stay
 and keep right on
 Lovin' you

I may take to the city
I may find a farm
 it might be cold
 it might be warm

 But I'll keep on
 Lovin' you

I may leave with first sunrise
hitch a ride with no goodbyes
 take my dreams to the open road
 hoping you know why I had to go
 and keep right on
 Lovin' you

My life is fulla mights and maybes
city country cold warm
 but one thing I know for true
leavin' stayin' comin' goin'
 I'll keep on
 Lovin' you

A Woman Left Lonely

She did not beg forgiveness.
she did not cry, scream, pout, nor point out
that he could not afford to throw stones.
she just made a quiet smile,
touched a lone fingertip to a single tear
rappelling his left cheek.
she sat close to him on their love seat.
sat close enough for their thighs to touch,
and said in that soft, reassuring voice of hers.
"we can get through this, if you're sure, you really want to.
I'm sorry that you found out the way you did.
I'm sorry that I had to step out on you.
I never want to hurt you,
but I don't have any confessions about how glad I am,
that I no longer have to live a lie.
the lie is what I had been living......before now.
I'm no child; I knew what I was doing.
there was no spite involved.
I was not seduced; I was rescued.
In addition to being your woman,
& a damn good one, according to you,
I am also human. I think you forgot that.
and I was lonely, and I needed love, your love.
I needed touching, your touch. I needed you.
But you were so busy being so successful
at all the things you're so damn good at anyway,
that you never took time (to take time) to notice,
that for the last few months, I just haven't been myself.
But now I am."
And he understood...And she stood up....And he cried.

I Need To Talk

Some mornings
after a night with you
dawn comes too quickly
interrupting illicit liaisons
enforcing curfews
swiftly rolling up darkness
like a stolen Monet
hastily cut from its frame
and stuffed into a hollowed cane
to be hidden away
in a cramped space
until night fall
next Tuesday

BUSTED
(PART ONE)

Some men like to brag about
 how long they can make love.
  But does it really matter
   how long you work on a car
    if you can't get it to run right?

One man liked to boast that he
 could make love from one day to the next.
  He even got his embarrassed wife
   to corroborate his braggadocio.

Late one evening,
 she confided to one of the ladies
  that the man isn't lying.
   He can go from one day to the next.

You see, he works the 4 p.m. to 11 shift.
 I always wait up for him.
  He's home by 11:30, showered by 11:50,
   & in bed by 11:55 or a few minutes later.

So if we start getting down
 around 11:58 or 11:59 p.m.
  that is, technically, one day.
   And if he's through by 12:01 a.m.,
    technically, that is another day.

So you see, he ain't lying.
 We often have sex lasting
  from one day to the next,
   but not in the way, he implies.

BUSTED
(PART TWO)

She said, "divorce is not an option
unless you want to bleed"
she had just one suggestion
O man was I relieved

She said, "let's renew our vows"
though we were on shaky ground
she had found out, who knows how
about my fooling around

She said, "I hope you used protection
for pregnancy and V.D."
she never had not one infection
not a single STD

She made appointments for us
I hadn't prayed that hard in years
I cried, when our labs came back
and Doc said, "you're in the clear"

I was on thin ice but she was nice
until I stuck out my hand
she slid two rings upon my finger
called me, her two-timing man

ESTRANGLED

Why do we,
why should we,
lie here in our king sized bed,
a bed empty of intimacy?
We lie here, interred, separated by inches,
yet, miles and worlds apart.

Why allow microscopic particles of despondency
to waft through unscreened retorts,
and snuggle like dust mites
which settle in the moats of emptiness
that isolate us from the love
that once ruled our castle?

Our polite coldness triggers OCD episodes. They keep our hands and hearts from touching. And our hearts, Oh, our hearts...if only there were angiograms to identify the blockages and angioplasty procedures to open cold broken hearts, if our insurances refused to pay on grounds of pre-existing conditions, I would find the funds to fix us.

Meanwhile, our hearts duet their hardening, and our hands, oh, how they ache to touch. They ache with a rheumatoid arthritic ache that neither ibuprofen, heat, steroids, yoga, acupuncture, nor massage can alleviate. I no longer remember why or when we decided not to touch, or if we decided at all. But it is not good for us, this strain which does not let us make eye contact nor ask or accept the slightest favor at all.

At supper, you rose from your seat and walked around the table to get the pepper, which I would have gladly handed to you.

What happened to us? Did I reach for you and you pulled away? Did I, hungry for hurt, need no explanation which might deprive me of a hurriedly thrown together, rush-to-judgment, last minute pity party?

Was a touch from you ignored, discarded by a look of disinterest or greeted with ambivalence? Sadly, I do not know. Do you? What I do know is, I would love it if our shoulders somehow managed to bump as we pass in our hallways, before carefully turning aside so even our sleeves refuse to touch. What I do know is, I would not mind at all if an errant toenail raked my leg as we politely avoid even accidental contact.

No longer soul-mates, now, we are cellmates, in this king size coffin that once was our personal and perfect idyllic island of mature passions.

Now, it is 42 sq. feet of solitary confinement, barely six feet across and no more than 7 feet long, yet, skin has not grazed skin in months on end. "Touch me! Please, just touch me! Somewhere! Touch anywhere," we cry out silently, telepathically. Tonight, even your perpetually cold feet could warm my heart if they would just touch me.

If we could retrieve the wasted moments and add them to the ends of our lives like hidden fees concealed in the fine print of a shady contract, until it is too late to back out. Caveat emptor.

If we could do this impossible possibility, maybe we could live forever, or at least long enough to learn to love again.

If we could announce a factory recall on every negative emotion issued in anger or sequestered in the volatile silence of self-imposed gag orders.

If we could target every nanosecond misspent in secret cutting sessions, as we carefully cut one another down to size, and maim deep, hurtful wounds into each other's souls, with putrid words, murderous looks, precursors to these unattended bedsores and ulcerous festering sorrows which defile us.

If only we could backspace, click "delete" or call "do over." If we could TiVo the madness, fast forward or rewind to the last or next smile. If I could only let my 3rd-eye be first to blink, and end this childish stare down, while obvious overtures go unopened, unread, un-rsvp'd, like so much junk-mail piling up on an old cocktail table.

Your left hand rests openly, deliberately outstretched, conveniently exposed atop the covers in the neutral zone which separates us. Your perfectly manicured hand, palm upturned, innocent, inviting, readily available, if my stubborn touch sought yours. And yet, we each wait for the other to bridge the gap, to cross the DMZ and be first to touch, to surrender and end this insane stalemate.

We continue lying-in-state, enshrouded in Egyptian Cotton, 1000 thread count, embalmed by malaise, locked in "Until death do we part" mortal combat.

We lie here, mummified by unforgiveness, pushing all the right buttons to get all the wrong things started again.

How long shall we remain filled and fueled by this embryonic hatred, or a fear of love, a fear more toxic than these slivers of hatred forced beneath thin skin like slivers of bamboo forced under fingernails.

In our blindness, we ceased to reason, ceased to realize that regardless of who or what reaches out first to touch, your toenail or my hand, when contact is made we have touched at the same time.

The instant my hand touches your wrist – your wrist touches my hand. Your toenail rakes my leg as my leg touches you. Why does it matter who brokers the peace as long as we are touching again?

Oh, foolish fools. Hurry! Embrace what is left of your love before it is too late, before the milk of human kindness curdles and fear hardens into a granite headstone in a previously unmarked grave in Potter's Field.

Touch her you fool. Touch her while she still wants to be touched by you. Touch her while her body language screams, "touch me, touch me now!"
Touch her you fool!
Touch her!
Touch!

MULTIPLE PERSONALITIES

You say you know
                    there's another woman
You say you can tell
                    by looking at me
But you'd never guess
                    that other woman
Is just the woman
                    you used to be

GROUNDS FOR DIVORCE

I still don't know how you did it,
but with everything you had going on at the time,
you, somehow, forgot we were in love.
you left me hanging like a cell-phone call
you never get back to
after a call-waiting interruption.
I understand, or rather I accept
that I slipped your mind
before you realized I was no longer holding on.

I have regrets, I won't lie,
but none which outweigh the heart murmurs
and the delicacies of x-rated intimacies
which I, too briefly, knew with you.
I am philosophical.
I don't know how long Lazarus lived
after Jesus raised him from the dead.
You resurrected me.
I'm still here; I'm still alive.
Your smile deep-tissue massaged my libido.
Your touch spread rumors and tremors
of reconciliation.
You drew me out of hiding,
lured me out of hibernation,
prematurely,
like a housefly hoodwinked
by unseasonably warm days.

We made news and set records that March
when temperatures fluctuated by 60 degrees
in 24 hours.
Too late, I realized, it is still winter
and I have not heard your voice this year.
there is so much I cannot say to you.
I am ten weeks overdue with pregnant pauses.
tomorrow is the anniversary of my birth date.
the official unveiling of Spring is only weeks away
and I have yet to hear your voice this year.

sure, we text, we type (TTYL, LOL, BTW, OMG, etc.).
I strain to hear your voice's sweet inflections
in the cold, silent, unfeeling keystrokes substituting
for the unparalleled eroticism of the spoken word.

sterile thumbs fly across q-w-e-r-t-y keyboards
of some smart-ass-I-phone.
I have this medical condition.
there is treatment but no cure.
I suffer sensory deprivation. When I love,
I need to see, hear, taste, touch and talk.
I am unabashedly old fashion, old skool,
or maybe, just plain old.

I am not some Sudoku-solving cyber-senior
with an e-book library card and 27 forgotten passwords.

I can't tweet what I feel for you.
I can't e-mail, Facebook, MySpace, this place
I have in my heart for you.

I am not high-tech. I am a hands-on man,
and reading and texting
these (I love U2's & xx's & oo's)
are like making love.

while wearing a 6-ply Bridgestone radial condom
with reinforced sidewalls guaranteed
to cancel the feel of any and all bumps and grinds.

Our love poem before this
had a full-bodied bouquet,
like a real kitchen with real sounds,
and real people with real laughter,
and real smells like homemade breads,
rolls, biscuits, and tiny cinnamon loaves
baked in mama's pans meant for her cornpones.

The poem before this one was vibrant,
alive with organic, orgasmic aromas
no lab-animal tested
olfactory inducements added
like the scents
of Febreze, Lysol, Pinesol,
or a 3.4 oz. spray bottle of Pheromones
or Paloma Picasso.

Now, our love is a silent film with foreign subtitles.
The lighting is poor. My reading speed is not good
and neither is my Spanish. I don't see so well
without my rose-tinted graduated bifocals,
and all I can make out in this light
is Adios.

Split Decision:
I'm Outta Here

When truth began to come out,
feelings were hurt,
yet, healings were transplanted like young shoots
set out in early Spring,
(fully compliant with the Farmer's Almanac).
"Let sleeping dogs lie," my mother cautioned.
"They have been lying long enough," my father said.
She continued to crochet.
He continued to fill the living room
with the sweet aroma of pipe tobacco.
Their combined advice,
seldom sought and never hurriedly given,
impaled me upon the brevity and wit of it.
Clutching their ten words like a meaty bone
snatched from bigger dogs by the runt of the litter,
I crouch in the cover of tall brush
to gnaw over their ten words.
"Let sleeping dogs lie.
They have been lying long enough."

It is as clear as clear can get,
I need more than I'm getting from you.
Knowing you as I do,
I find it hard to believe, no, impossible to believe
that you are holding back on me.

I have been cheating on myself.
I have been pushing on a door marked **Pull,**
and it is never going to open that way.
I am tired of feeding my soul on leftovers.

I am a grown man, 180 pounds plus,
I can't make it on the 600-800 calories of affection
which you dole out so begrudgingly.
You're killing me with my consent,
or as Brother Namon Arnold puts it,
"I am stuck in a slightly comfortable nightmare."
If you had not done what you did, I may never
have noticed that I do not love you.
My true feelings took me by surprise.
They startled me like a resting raccoon nestled in an
open rural mail box, that I reach into without looking.
Until that day, I thought I loved you,
and it wasn't as though I stopped loving you that day.

As my words poured out, carrying my hurt away,
carrying it as a clogged drain suddenly freed
from the dirt and debris that had slowly built up
over the years and blocked its once natural flow.
Only then did I realize,
I could not pinpoint the day, week, month or year

that I quit loving you, my Dear.

And yes, I am fully aware that I am doing
some pretty nifty, emotional, back peddling.
You're absolutely right. I am reneging on
all promises given,
all pledges made, and every syllable of
my "until death do we part" vow foolishly taken.
Well, a death has occurred; it should be investigated as a
homicide, but I don't care about that now.

Like the poem Gilded Butterfly stated:
"You killed the love I had for you;
you rationed the very air I breathe.
We both did wrong, you're not just to blame,
but now, I must be free."

My love for you flat-lined on your watch.
I don't even know the time of death.
While you were on duty, cries of "stat" and "code blue"
went unheeded and unheard.
While I gasped for your tenderness,
you surfed the internet,
changed your Facebook profile
and updated your status.
Well, here's something new you can add:
recently single, newly divorced, flat broke.
I was love starved; you refused to feed me.
I laugh as I remember a few lines I recently read,

"Once, we were the perfect pair.
I was the kind of man who asked for nothing,
and you were the kind of woman who gave it."

So my darling,
and I call you that for the last time in this life time.
I'm going to do something for you
that the devil never did.
I'm going to leave your sorry ass alone.

So vaya con Dios, if God will have you.
And vaya con Diablo, if He won't.
Either way, I'm outta here.
Adios.

O
Woman
when
my
friends
ask
me
if
I
still
miss
you,
why
do
I
always
lie
O
Woman

O WOMAN
(GPS)

excuse me
I'm new in town
even though I almost grew up here
(one fall semester)
everything is so different now
or is it simply I who have changed
either way
I need your help
I've been driving around for hours
going in circles......doing the man-thing
not asking for directions
telling myself I'm not really lost
but that shit ain't working any longer
not for me nor my gas gauge
my tank's on "E"
it's Sunday evening in small town America
they have rolled up the sidewalks
it's after dark and I need your help
just between you and me,
I'm as lost as Columbus
so if you don't mind
would you please
show me the best way
back to your heart
O Woman

My Special Friend

Do you think of me when certain songs play
or when you feel a familiar sadness
and wish there was someone you could talk to,
someone who would not try to heal your hurt
or shush your tears with new age affirmations

someone to just listen and let you vent and flow
when what you need most is to hurt for a while,
to wrap yourself in warm weariness,
to snuggle up in cozy misery, to curl up in self-pity
and fight to keep the tears flowing,
as though you know that you can cry away
the last of the hurt, and for awhile, live again?

Do you think of us when you see other couples
holding hands, hugging, kissing, laughing, loving,
or arguing some point that is not nearly as important
as the simple enjoyment of matching wits in a friendly debate
about something of worth or nothing at all?

Do you think of us when some movie comes on
that we hugged up to and watched years ago,
when I never dreamed I would ever be without you?
Do you ever watch wrestling or re-runs of *"All In The
Family,"* for old time's sake?

Do you ever pull out your "dusties," your Ol' school jams, we
used to listen to, and deejay a private pity party
late into the night ? Do you choke back tears at Roberta Flack's,
"The First Time Ever I Saw Your Face"? I do. I just did.

I could cry this very moment, and wrap myself
in a familiar, warm, cozy, sadness. I miss you like crazy.

Do you still have the love letters I wrote back in the day, with
postmarks dating back to the early 70's, when postage stamps
were eleven cents? If so, do you take them out and reread and
relive those days when love was all that mattered? I do. And to
make matters worse or maybe better, the scented stationery you
used still emits a fragrance made sweeter by the years. Did you
do that deliberately so that the bouquet of you could haunt me
or bless me forever? What fragrance lasts for 40 years? Yours'
has. I never married, so there was no one to demand that I get
rid of the evidence that once I loved and was loved in, with, and
for every fiber of my being.

Do you think of me on those frequent nights when sleep plays
hide-go-seek and insomnia keeps you company far too long? I
should have held on to you when I had you and you had me,
when I was in love and knew it and knew you knew. Why did
you let me let you go? Why didn't you make me see that we
were meant to be together? You were the brains of the outfit. I
was only the Poet.

Do you write longhand letters to me, though you can't possibly
know my address, only to tear them up when that day's
emptiness leaves?

Do you search for me on Facebook, and Google my name in
vain? Do you miss me like I miss you? I sure hope you do.
My Special Friend.

Can I Say I'm Sorry

Can I say I am sorry
with no one to make me apologize
can I show her my regret
before the tears come to her eyes
Can I beg her to forgive me
before she knows that I've been wrong
can I appeal to her for mercy
because I hurt for what I've done

Can I show her I am sorry
for the pain I almost brought
can I beg for her forgiveness
Though I'm sure I won't be caught
Can I tell her I am sorry
though I did not cheat that day
but I went with good intentions
our vows to betray

Oh, I know how close I came
to crossing that cheating line
and it wounds me when she prays
thank you for this man of mine
I may lose her if I tell her
of what was almost done
but if I keep it from her
I know we are no longer one

"I don't know what she will do
but I can't worry about that now
I can only confess my sins and pray
she'll still be mine somehow."

WHAT IF

Let's suppose for argument's sake
　that love is really all it takes
　　to heal a hurting grown-up world
　　　of grown-up boys and grown-up girls
　　　Let's recall the times as a child
　　　　when kisses healed and brought a smile
　　　　O' was it real or make believe
　　　　　that hugs and kisses could relieve

A real scrape with blood and all
　from some scary playground fall
　　just tell Mommy where it hurts
　　　were words to make the medicine work
　　　In those days, we could not doubt
　　　　that Moms could kiss the pains all out
　　　　and Dads could scare the boogey-man
　　　　back into their boogey-land

So when did we become too old
　for hugs and kisses to console
　　and love away the grown-up tears
　　　who said wisdom comes with years
　　　Let's just suppose for argument's sake
　　　　that Love is really..............all it takes
　　　　to kiss and hug life's pains away
　　　　　it's recess time......you're it......Let's play

To The Women Who Love(d) Me
(Vous êtes très belle)

God gave me a secret love
He said to give to you
You did not know that He had sent
enough to see us through

You expected none at all
so I gave just part to you
Your smile said, "We are thrice blessed."
while the rest I held on to

And so it is so many times
we hold such loving back
then cry when hearts come up half full
and lie about the lack

God gave me a love for you
which is no longer mine
to try to act as though it is
is both a sin and crime

That loving you is what I do best
I used to feel it was a flaw
then you removed my cataracts
and a brand new world I saw

As I began to read to you
my court reporter notes
I found the answers which I sought
lay in the words I wrote

It was well-hidden treasure
concealed by guile and stealth
now found in no small measure
sitting right inside myself

And so it's kind of funny
or you may call it something else
but it is through my love for you
I've come to love myself

DREAMING
(TAPESTRY)

We should be lying
face to face this night
    I on my left side
    you on your right

    with my right leg
    thrown over both of yours

my right hand
should be stroking your left side
    carefully following each warm brown curve
    like an experienced grand-prix driver

  my kiss should be dipping
  into your every recess
    following the dark silhouette
    of your familiar breasts

    of your quivering hips rising
    above your moistened thighs

    like a golden sunrise

    I should be loving you.....this way
                this night
    but you are gone
    and I'm....................wet dreaming

DEJA-VU

O Woman
the Cyclops' eye
of a single exposed breast
peeks shyly through
your partially opened blouse
as you rest
your gentle snore
almost an afterthought of sleep
keeps a subdued beat
like the shuussh, shuussh
of brushes
tiptoeing across jazz cymbals
synchronized to the rise and fall
of your breath's muffled crescendo

a single nipple
bloodshot in the morning light
stares unblinking
at my darting tongue
it hovers
I harvest your fragrant nectar
the ceiling fan hums
slightly off key
or is it me?
O Woman

DEJA-VU
(DEUX)

...and does it sound cliché
                    to say
                    touché

I've passed
            this way before

does it sound cliché
                to say
                touché
                I know the score

                I've been in love
                at least,
                one time before

and I see smiles
where others say
                there's only space
                I would know you anywhere
                how could I, forget that face

It's so damn nice
happening into you
                how have you been
                my ol' friend

                Deja-vu

...and as for me
I've been deeply in love
where I knew right away

     that I would never love
     that way again
     yes, I've been there before
     and I've been back again

what a coincidental
     rendezvous
          fancy runnin' into you
          my ol' friend

          Deja-vu

the way you interpret
just-uh fleeting stage-of-life
     makes me almost remember
     who I met you through

     well,
     so long
     til then
     see you later, my friend
        Godspeed to you
        have a nice time
        take care
        and peace to you
        'til we meet again

        my ol' friend
        Deja-vu

To Cynthia M. Koroma

O Woman
do me a favor
the next time you're leaving town
just go
don't let me know; keep it under your hat,
unless you're taking me with you
Knowing you are leaving
makes the skies a little dimmer,
makes each night a little longer,
makes Chicago a little emptier,
and me.................a little colder
so next time.....just go
We will continue our daily talks,
or every other day-or-so chats,
texts, and emails
I will have no way of knowing
that you are not nestled snugly
in your bungalow on South Emerald,
tightly curled into
one of your favorite fetal positions,
cover pulled over head,
phone wedged between ear-&-shoulder,
hands sandwiched between knees,
your sultry voice,
deliciously channeling Nina Simone
Upon your return
you can call and say:

"Hey, guess what?
For the last six days
I've been in Idaho Falls,
or Alpharetta, Georgia,
or Portsmouth, N.H.,
or a little piece of Heaven
just outside of San Diego."
We will laugh
You will tell me all about it
I will thank you
for leaving the lights on
in my Chicago,
while you were so far away
Thanks again,
for leaving the lights on
and the door cracked
I love you for that
O Woman

TAMARA

Tamara
last night
you were northern lights
filling mid-western skies
shining over the south-side
Continent of Chicago
like my personal aurora borealis

If I were not a Poet
I would become one
just to see your face and 300 Watt eyes
light up and sparkle in September
or any month where you are appearing
You are as infectious as Ebola
contagious as playground laughter
and oh so soothing
soothing as a good mother's kisses
spread generously on a hurt
Spread all thick and sweet and good-gooey
like tupelo honey
dripped on
an open-faced whole wheat
organic peanut butter sandwich

Ooops
I think I just made me
hunger for you
O Woman

In Memory of Marion Joyce Baker
& 333 E. 26th Street

It was 1967 B.C. (before cell-phones)
I was 19 and crazy in love, or just crazy
depending on who you talked to
and I was in love with Joyce
I lived at 4437 South Indiana Avenue
on the south side of Chicago
in a single room, misnamed Apartment 5
of a 3rd floor, walk-up, not-too-hip tenement
with community kitchen and bath
and walking distance from Gladys' Restaurant
and I was in love with Joyce
but sometimes, I was more in love than other times
and at other times she was
and in the times when she wasn't a whole lot
in love with me
I would be at home waiting
for her to come over like she had promised
and I would turn out the lights
and lie in the dark and try to sleep
so the time would pass faster
and when the doorbell would ring
I would hold my breath and pray
that it would ring 5 times for Apartment No. 5
but most of the time it didn't
and you know, it's a fucking drag
counting to four, then holding your breath
for that 5th ring
that doesn't come

WHO IS SHE?

Neither Playboy
    nor Penthouse
ever saw poses like yours
so innocent,
so natural, they cannot be called nudes

no air brush necessary; no photo-shop
no spray bottles ready to fabricate
perfect beads of water
         cascading

            d

             o

              w

               n

                the valley
          be...tween your breasts
drip................ping into the recessed cave mouth
                 of your hidden navel
Neither Playboy
    nor Penthouse
    ever dreamed there was a centerfold masterpiece
    when you emerged from the waterfall
        of an ancient shower head
which sent its cockeyed spray
      s c u r r y i n g in every direction
you sat your ample bottom on a thick towel
folded double and placed without fanfare

——an ancient souvenir from the 5-star hotel
   whose beds you made, yet, never laid upon——
your paints clamor around you
like beggar children awaiting a hand-out
——an uncut loaf of bread, a wedge of cheese,
   fresh strawberries, and a bottle of Merlot
   could complete the photo shoot,
   (if there were one)
   and place you on the banks of the Seine,
   or River Thames
But not today.....today
you take something, I shall just call them lady-things
they looked like brass knuckles made of foam
you place them between the toes of each foot

you draw your left heel onto the bed,
expertly survey the bottled colors:
apple green, midnight purple,
yellow, plum, copper, pink,
red n' red, peacock blue,
displayed on your canopied queen sized palette

your Sistine chapel beckons;
you begin to paint
your toe nails become your canvas,
your self-commissioned mural
you begin to create

you pose for no cameras,
primp for no audience,
present....nor....future
you simply paint your toenails
    you wear no makeup
    no rings, not even an earring

your jewelry is made of flesh:
priceless breasts,
adorned with exquisite nipples,
centered and set in the areola shade

    perfectly placed oases of soft wet hair,
    stretch mark tattoos blend perfectly
    across your lower belly,
    a tribute to the fruit you bore

a birth mark that resembles nothing but a birth mark
    brands an inch or so of your left shoulder,
    as if some life spilled on you and soaked in,
    before it could be wiped away without smudging

    you wore no clothes not made of flesh,
    and yet, you were not nude; you were not naked;
    you were not in the buff; you were not au-naturel

    you were a woman who came home from work,
    took a long, hot, relaxing bath,
    showered the excess soap from your full figure,
    then sat to do your nails,

while I worked around your work,
gently massaging African Shea butter
into your available parts
    I softly blow-dry your coochie-brunette hair
    with my breath
    They never saw it coming

    Eat your hearts out..........Guccione and Hef

Street Lady

I can't give you
anything
    but pure love
    come storm or rain
    and still I want you
My goal is not
the dollar bill
    only love
    can bring the thrill
    I get from you

Street walking lady
woman-child
    I wish that you would stay awhile
    and let love grow
This 50 dollars that I spend
can't compare
    to what's within
    my heart for you
But you're a Lady
of the street
    and currency
    is all you seek
    to get from me
So I'll admire you
from afar
    and love you just
    the way you are
    one night a week
    My precious Lady
    of the street

THE HOOKER
(IN HER 20's)

She never dreamed that someday
she'd stand alone on the street
selling herself from day to day
for shelter, food, and drink

Yesterday, she was a happy woman
no thoughts of being alone
today she's an empty embittered soul
her loving man is gone

It's cold and lonely trying to live
hiding her broken heart
and for a time cheap alcohol
helped her play the part

Each day another man comforts her
driving the pain away
Time after time they come to love
but never come to stay

And now each night she's out there
half-shadowed in the dark
finishing out a broken life
inside a broken heart

The Hooker
(IN HER 30's)

Each night she silently leaves the lounge
to go and take her stand
She knows with a little luck tonight
she'll find a spending man
Beneath the dimly glowing lights
we can see her take her place
and always that searching look
upon her painted face

She looks as if she knows each man
They pause, she raises a brow.
Two years ago, she'd never dreamed
she'd be The Hooker now

So all alone she stands there
Her face is made of stone
No matter how the crowds may surge
she stands out all alone

And there she is just a shell
on market to any man
She waits in life, neither coming or going
just accepting what she can

She wonders at the plans she had
for setting ablaze this world
But now she's seen this bitter place twice
an old woman, while still a girl

The "for sale" look in her eyes
her face is etched with lines
She searches the face of every man
hoping for the sign

Her straight life is all but faded
Other plans are in their place
And now there's just that haunted look
upon her painted face

THE HOOKER
(IN HER 40's)

Her smile answered, they disappear
embraced in the knowing dark
He'll never know, she'll never show
the emptiness of her heart

To everyone she's without pain
with her we unload our strife
A bottle, a story, another man
Is this The Hooker's life?

She doesn't really live there
under the yellowed lights
It is only there we find her
seeking our refuge in the night

And even as she stands waiting
The Hooker makes her plans
A home, a family, but right now
another spending man

And now the money changes
from hand to waiting hand
She gives and then she's off to find
another spending man

And for weeks she'll be there standing
so alone and in her place
the lines deepen, the hopes lessen
The fear grows on her face

THE HOOKER
(IN HER 50's)

Her face is riddled with signs of sorrow
the smile, it's still in place
but now it's like a crimson gash
across her weathered face

The looks now go unanswered
the fear pulls at her breast
the age shows, the men know
this one is past her best

And now all night she's out there
too old, but not ashamed to try
Hoping and praying, searching the faces
but no one wants to buy

Although she knows her day is gone
she smiles, still raising a brow
but younger girls are on her corner
playing The Hooker now

But still, she's always out there
old and broken she takes her stand
And hopes in vain tonight she'll find
Her Biggest............Spending Man

Do You Remember?

There was nothing casual
about our sex,
and I ain't talking gender
We made love the first night we met
And I ain't just talking 'bout having sex
Later, you asked,
"Is this a one night stand?"
"Well," I replied, "That's kinda up to you
It all depends on what you are doing
tomorrow night."

There was nothing causal about our sex
it was loud, intense, frenetic
bold, explosive, experimental
drug, liquor, lust and love induced
inner-city safaris
into unchartered seas and seizures of ecstasy.
we don't get down like that anymore
you found religion
though at times we call to resurrect the old days
and laugh about how we used to do blow
and study the Bible without a hint of hypocrisy
that was 30-some years ago
now, we bump into each other by accident
we call on birthdays, we are both March Pisces
and I still know your old number by heart

(773) 555-
Naw, I can't reveal the rest. Let them guess

High Love Pressure

There was nothing causal about our sex
we met through a mutual freek.
Note the spelling f-r-e-e-k
he cleared it with you to give me your number
I called; we talked; I made love poetry to you over the phone
Eight/nine/ten poetic climaxes. we lost count
you gave me your address; I came by
you said you wanted to buy my latest book
I was impressed that a fine young thing like you
owned her own home. I was a nomad poet in those days, a
psychedelic troubadour
I had a car, but I house-pooled,
a few nights here, a few nights there,
but my mail went to my folks place. that's where I called
home. that's where I always had keys to the front door and
could open the fridge without asking
you were dark chocolate, I had a sweet tooth,
and a sudden craving for chocolate covered cherry
you were in the health profession in those days
you were working the graveyard shift
you excused yourself to go upstairs
to put the finishing touches on your exit routine
you descended minutes later;
I had the Book-of-Joe in one hand and me in the other
"What.......what is this?" you gasped! Is that for me?"
"Which?" I asked, as my gaze fell to my filled hands
"Both," you said. You called off work that night,
30-some years ago
And I still know your number by heart
(773) but back in those days, it was (312) 555-6???
Naw, I can't reveal the rest. Let them try to guess

REFLECTIONS

A Randy Travis Song

If the bad times
really make the good times
that much better
that much better
then this time
it should be
that much better-rrr..........than before
for you and I
we've had our bad times
that's for sure...................that's for sure
We had more than
our share of hard times
yet, somehow
we kept holding on
to the truth.....................and one another
and like they say
the darkest hour
is just...............before dawn
keep holding on........................keep holding on
Sometimes, it seemed
like we'd go under
but that's the time
we'd come on strong
now, here we are
and still together
the night has gone
here's the dawn
Keep holding on.....................Keep holding on

35TH CLASS REUNION

Why did I never say "I do"
to any of the loves I knew
Was I so blind to love's suggestion
or just afraid to pop the question

They say hindsight is 20/20
and yes, I have looked back aplenty
and through the eyes of retrospect
have seen the sunset genuflect

And bow to unrequited love
which I was so damn unsure of
revealed by some wrong word I spoke
or some silence which shyness invoked

But I cannot allow and let
a second 40 years of regret
use introversion as excuse
who needs to talk? I have my muse

Time heals all wounds is a myth
I waive my rights to plead the fifth
and take the stand to testify
I love you still, and that's no lie

And will…until the day I die!
And maybe longer…if I try!

At Seventeen

At seventeen, if someone said to me
I would love this way at sixty-three
I would have laughed, you must be joking
pass me some of what you're smoking

At seventeen, if I were told
I'd love this way when I was this old
would I've received it as prophecy
or just some harmless lunacy

You see my friends, it's not too late
for love comes with no "use by" date
it does not spoil nor lose its flavor
for age can only improve its savor

Don't listen as round you rumors fly
whispering "love has passed you by"
he said, she said, not a thread of proof
idle hearsay, not a shred of truth

For love is neither fad nor fashion
it is much more than lust and passion
suppose for the sake of argument
that love is really....Earthly rent

That Love is really........Heaven sent

NEVER TOO OLD
(NOV. 3, 2011)

You may be too old for playing hop-scotch
or for crying to get things your way
you may be too old to run tattle-tale
every secret you hear someone say

You may be too old for Red Rover, Red Rover
or going outside at lunchtime to play
you may be too old for double-dutch & jacks
hide-n-seek, and Simon Says, someday

You may be too old to use fake I.D.'s
to sneak you and your buddies in a bar
you may be too old for backseat romancing
and for pretending you're more than you are

You may be too old to let friends tag along
when you go meet your "Love-at-first-sight"
you may be too old to need their approval
when it's someone.........you really like

You may be too old for dyeing your hair
red, orange, green, purple, and blue
but how can you say, you're too old for love
When Love ....is much older.......than you

You may be too old for "double-dog-dare-you"
or for making-out down by the lake
you may be too old for wearing tight clothes
or telling friends how much money you make

You may be too old to play spin-the-bottle
or "pinky swear," like you used to do
you may be too old to go skinny-dipping
too old, and too self-righteous, too

You may be too old to stay all night drinking
much more than you know you should drink
you may be too old to spend your time thinking
much about....................what others may think

You may be too old to follow the crowd
and do whatever crowd-followers do
you may be too old for Red-light/Green-light
playing tag........and bikes.........built for two

You may be too old to take one more chance
to make all your day-dreams come true
But how can you say, you're too old for love
When love's...........so much older.......than you

SECOND WIND

I thought I'd never love again
the hourglass had poured her sand
I, calloused by a life of hurt
never thought the glass to invert

And bid the sadness all adieu
erase the slate and start anew
but I had not the inner strength
to halt the hurt, then at length

You appear from God knows where
in answer to an unknown prayer
and turning the glass right side up
proceed my sadness to disrupt

I thought I'd never love again
but you my friend had other plans
and with a charm you drew me in
and rubbed new life into my skin

And over protests of unsolved pain
you challenged me to love again
and for the first time in years
my life was not about the fears

But now about new hopes and dreams
and fantasies of useful things
like days of joy.................as never before
O God, it's good............to love once more

That's What Good Love Do

no strings attached
is how she loves me
no strings attached
is how she cares

and I may never
fall in love
forever, any more
no strings attached
no things to snatch
that's the score

no strings attached
is how I hold her
no strings attached
is how we care

and we may never
fall in love
forever
ever again
no strings attached
no schemes to hatch
that's the plan

Her Special Day

This year, this time,
why not write her a love poem?
So what, if you are not a Poet.
It doesn't have to be a literary Tour-de-Force.
And read it to her.
It doesn't matter if your voice is not the timbre
of a James Earl Jones' baritone.
Hold her hand while she reads it back to you.
Write her a love song.
Sing it to her in that off key voice of yours,
like you used to do,
when you hardly knew her and she barely knew you.
In your regular voice,
let your awkward words of love stutter and stumble
from your insecure tongue.
Embarrass yourself if you must.
She will love you all the more for it.
Replace Hallmark's perfect verse
whose massed produced words can never be yours.

Think about it. Right now, in stores across the country,
thousands of unsure spouses and lovers
roam aisle after aisle, reading card after card,
in search of that special one which says
what we think our loved ones need to hear.
But not this time.

This time, let's not fall prey to cookie-cutter exact,
straight from the heart,
special occasion confessions,
perfect serenades,
penned by professionals,
paid for by corporations,
published for profit,
to do our sweet talking for us.
Maybe someday, but not today, not this time.

Now, I ain't hating. More than one greeting card, and
more than one sweet love song have put in a good word for me.
I know your Lady loves her some:
Luther Vandross,
some Teddy Pendergrass,
some Marvin Gaye,
some Anthony Hamilton,
some Al Green,
some Jaheim,
some Maxwell,
some Brian McKnight,
some Usher,
some Robin Thicke,
some Jill Scott,
some India Arie,
some Erykah Badu,

some Alicia Keyes,
and for sure,
some Sade.

But not this time.
This time, be your own Cyrano de Bergerac
This time, speak for yourself.
Quote your heart to her.
It is you she loves,
not the flowers, cards, candies, and jewels.
It is you she wants to receive.
In addition to the gifts you've given over the years,
she can and has bought many of her own diamonds,
chocolates, cars, and cruises.
But it is you she loves, not the things. Don't you know
that your words & arms are hearth & home to her?
It is you she wants to feel.

You would not think to hire a Casanova,
far more gifted in the art-of-making-love
than you ever hope to be,
and pay him
to make unbelievable love to your Queen,
as your way of letting her know
how deeply you care,
and how much you want to see her pleased
in **every** way.
No way. It ain't gonna happen!
So save the slow jams.

Tonight, be your own "Smooth Operator."
Sade can sing later.
Release what comes to your heart.
Believe me, it will come out right
because she loves you.
Give me a chance to say, "I told you so."
Luther can't hold her. Maxwell can't phone her.
This is one case Johnnie Cochran couldn't argue for you.
You must throw caution to the wind.
You must take the stand and testify on your own behalf.
You, must represent love.
She is not Hallmark's Lady. She is your Queen!
Allow your closing remarks to open the door to your heart.
Let her see more deeply into you, than ever before.
Open the windows of your soul.
Let the radiance of your expanding love for her
illuminate both lives and cast angelic shadows
on soon-to-be busy boudoir walls.
Stand naked, guileless before your Queen.
Do you swear to tell the Truth, the whole Truth,
and nothing but the Truth,
so help you Love?
"I Do."

The Ladies' Room

O Woman
when marooned
in a public bathroom
and you must tinkle (as you ladies like to call it),
you all don't even think about "number two"
you levitate your beautiful behind
to hover weightless, inches above
some foreign toilet seat.
.........you would just as soon eat off its floor
as to let your perfect derriere
even slightly graze the petri dish,
of this indoor outhouse.
as you go into your yoga half squat,
visualize the hidden camera
of my unrepentant imagination,
conjuring naked images,
rotating, changing angles,
whirring, zooming in to catch you
as you pull your secret stash of
emergency toilet paper from your handbag,
now safely clutched between chin-&-chest
to avoid contamination of the crime scene.
after releasing a long satisfying stream
punctuated by a long satisfying aaahhhhhh,
you dry the residual pubic dew
from your thighs' once busy intersection

"Here, you missed a drop;
allow me to assist you,"

(I commune telepathically)
you pat your well-coiffed
bikini-waxed hairs into place
as though they are actually appearing
in the real life *Vagina Monologues*
when we hook up this evening.

you pull your panties up;
wiggle your skirt down
over full, naturally tanned hips.
you bump open the stall door with your elbow
(thank God, it swings outward; that's unusual).
you step, lady-like, back into the common area
of a less than inviting powder room.
you clean your hands with your ever present
antibacterial hand sanitizer,
with moisturizers & vitamin E.
you check yourself in the smudged mirror.
a wad of toilet paper protects you
from the unsavory door handle as you leave.

"why can't we pee like men?" you mumble,
as you pull the door and make your exit.

well,

that's a wrap............film at eleven.

INNOCENCE

Don't say that.
Daddy ain't drunk.
He just stood up too fast
and his legs got dizzy.

To Mamma Betty (Flowery)

My love is a warm weather flower
Which cannot bloom in cold
But Girl, you have the power
To make my bloom unfold

Just water me with your kisses
To prune my thorns away
And if a drop or two misses
I'll bloom for you, anyway

WOMAN CHILD
(BLACK ODYSSEY)

get up mama
the babies been fed
the beds been made
   and that new uncle
   you brought home last night

   I saw him
   slippin' outta here
   carrying your purse
   'bout six this morning

get up mama
the hairs been braided
the socks been mated

   and Tanya can't start school
   less'n you come with her
   on her first day

   so get up mama
   so she don't be late

Reprinted From:
One Room Shack

I want to grind corn and make bread
and walk through grassy fields at 6 a.m.
I want to cut trees and build with my hands
and raise a vegetable garden
I want to climb trees and look into birds' nests
and skip barefooted down dirt roads
I want to gulp cool water from the pump's mouth
and read novels by kerosene lamp
I want to glance worriedly at the skies
and wonder if the roof will leak again tonight
I want to watch newborn puppies nuzzling for milk
and see leopard frogs perched on lily pads
I want to peer out of cracked windows
and wait for someone special to appear
I want to hold someone for hours
and not make love
I want to do simple things
and be human again
I want to

Renaissance Woman:
Cousin Carol

I was glad for her,
When she told me she was moving.
I was glad for her and maybe,
just a little sad for me.
We had not been friends for long,
only twelve years or so,
but we were the kind of friends
who actually saw each other face-to-face,
several times a month, maybe more.
Ours was no Facebook friendship. We were
definitely on the backside of the digital divide.
We talked more than we text.
We always laughed when one would call to say,
"Hey, I just text you;
check it out and get back to me."
Like I said, I was glad
when she said she was moving.
It was where she said she was moving
that threw me for a loop.
(Especially since it was not job or man related)
I said to her,
"Atlanta, I could understand, or Chicago,
maybe even Miami, possibly Boston,
most definitely L.A., maybe Philly,
perhaps D.C., Seattle, Spokane, or Richmond,
On a smaller scale:

Charlotte, Orlando, Minneapolis,
Toronto, Providence, Memphis, New Orleans,
maybe even Biloxi,
But Butte, Montana! Butte, Montana?
Who the hell do you know in Butte, Montana?"
"I know me." she replied. "I know me."

In Memory of MJB
(1947–1994)

No one knew me like you. You worried that I would quit you when I found out you were pregnant. I was 16, and still a virgin. You wanted to talk and could not find the nerve to tell me what you did not know I already knew. I took you downtown to the movies. The first was "The Satan Bug" with George Chakiris; the next was "The Train" with Frank Sinatra and Burt Lancaster, I think. After all, that was in 1964-or-65.

You worried that I would quit you once you told me you were pregnant. I worried that you were going to tell me you were pregnant, then quit me. But me, quit you? You were my only friend at Wendell Phillips, maybe in all of Chicago. You could have shown me evidence that you were planning to kill me later that night, and I still wasn't going anywhere.

You rescued me at Wendell Phillips in "64." At first, you made school bearable. Then you made life exciting. Later, you told me of all the girls you scared off. We laughed. I was wet behind the ears. You dried them. We worked at Spiegels, ate at H-&-H, and got our perms and conks at Style Town, on 43rd & Indiana. I remember, Alfonso Rollins, Gladys, you and I walking 47th Street in the Big snow of "67." We used to walk from Michigan to Oakenwald. Oakenwald was so bad in those days, that cabs were reluctant to pick up or drop off there. Joyce, we are supposed to be laughing about riding the jump-seat in Jitney cabs before South Park became King Drive. You are the reason

I wrote the poem, *"No matter how crazy a Brother drives, he can always find some girl to ride with him."* I was that driver. You were my girl. But Ol' Lou Gehrig's disease stole you from me in 1994, leaving me to grow old alone and reminisce, without you. Joyce, I love you still.

EARTH ANGEL:
FOR DAZALEE COFFEY

Have you ever met an Angel
and you knew it right away?
If not my friends just look right here
an Angel's on display.

One day, I met an Angel
I even saw her wings
for she flew on love so true
her thoughts became great things.

I even saw her halo
I bet you saw it too,
and mistook it for a charming weave
or just her new hairdo.

I even saw her flaming sword
never drawn in her defense,
unsheathed alone in the name of Love
for those who lacked the strength.

I wonder if she even knew
her divine identity,
for she was as down to earth my friends
as anyone you'll meet.

And even now, I feel thrice blessed
As she turns Seventy,
for one day I met Earth's Angel

Whom I call Dazalee.

A Tribute To Annie Lee
(Inspired by JoAnn Griffin & Tiscur)

She is our Norman Rockwell. Google her name.
She is artist-poet-storyteller.
She paints what the Harlem Renaissance poemed.
Her drawings, her paintings are hieroglyphics
on canvas ceilings and cave walls.
Her figurines are shadows cast by 3D images
she scratched into pyramid stone.

She-uh hunter. She capture spirit. Her a dream catcher. They
whisper, "Shush. Be quiet. We be safe. She allergic to oils."
They think they escape her.
She catch them anyway.
She hold them with pastel spells.
She performs CPR on our history's "dry bones."
Google her name. Gossip her vision.
She-uh urban anthropologist,
unearthing southern artifacts lost during
the great migration. She excavate Asiatic bones:
Holy Ghost, 60 Pounds, Hot Water Cornbread,
Seeds N' Rinds, Sprinkling and Pressing, Fish Heads,
Blue Monday. Who don't know 'bout Blue Monday?

Who she anyway? Who this Annie Frances Lee?
Some whisper, when she paint,
she got that ancient veil over her face.
My Mama say my Grandmama had it too.

That Annie, she see what we don't,
not til her paint brush points out the poetry
in hot flashing, high-stepping, & jitter-bugging.
Poems like Personal Furnace, White Tie Only, RSVP,
Overheated, Bud and Lucille, Stage Door Exit.

Back in the day, if truth be told, back before
the Exodus, when she was in Glenwood, IL.,
I took my children out of school early one day.
"Annie Lee and Friends Gallery" was our Field trip.
I told the folk at Gavit Middle School that
she was a protector, a shaman priestess, a curator
of Kemetic History, a griot with a paint brush,
and my children must meet her, and get blessed,
before she leaves for Nazareth or Vegas.

"Queen Annie." That's what I call you
when I phone and you answer.
You bring much joy to your fans.
Yeah. You got fans. You our rock star.
I called one morning and gave the phone
to a young lady, every bit of 70 something.
She jumped and shouted like a little girl.
She screamed like they used to scream for Elvis.
But she was screaming for you. Her Annie Lee.
She could not believe she was talking
 to "The Annie Lee," as she put it.
She told you that you made her day. I was there.
You told her she made yours too. It made my day

to see you make her day, with just the sound of your voice,
healing her soul in Gary, Indiana, while you were in Texas.
That's what you mean to us.

Didn't y'all hear that Sister shouting?
Didn't you hear her Tyler Perry, Bill Duke?
Didn't you hear her John Singleton, Spike Lee?
Did you hear her Julie Dash, Oprah,
George Tillman, Jr., Tracey Edmonds?
Didn't y'all hear her? Didn't y'all hear that Sister shouting?
Tom Joyner heard her and he shouted.
And me, I'm still shouting. Detroit is shouting.
Is anyone Hollywooded-up enough
to whisper this icon's name to the big screen?
Can't a slight rewrite squeeze My Queen
between the breaking up, the making up,
and the chase scene, so some character gives or receives an
Annie Lee oil painting, lithograph or figurine? Although the
world and Texas have dibs on her,
she is a Chicago keepsake. She is Chicago,
a Wendell Phillips alum. She's as Chicago as Gwendolyn
Brooks, Melvin King, Haki Madhubuti,
Dr. Margaret Burroughs, The Chicago Defender,
the Jesse White Tumblers and the Bud Billiken Parade.
Annie Lee, She be the Windy City. She be Chi-town.

She be Maya Angelou with a paint brush.
Each figurine, each paperweight, each note card,
mug and magnet is a poem, a novella, an African Anthem of

American resurrection and redemption.

Annie Lee, your brush pours libations to "Mama.
Queen," "Sadie's Relief," "Mother's Board," "Gimme Dat Gum,"
"Mississippi Samsonite," "100% Cotton."

You were not the "1930's New Deal" we read about in history
books. You were and are the "Real Deal!" For years, you
quietly fed thousands. You waved your magic wand over
canvas. You made jobs for anyone who wanted to work. No
drug tests, no background checks, no b.s. We went to work
matting and selling "Annie Lee" note-cards while others waited
for government rescues that never came.

You planted your gifts. You sowed your art and entrepre-
neurs sprang up selling "Annie Lee" from homes, storefronts,
galleries, websites, shopping malls and flea market stalls.
We brainstormed. We burned midnight oils. We became busi-
ness men and women to meet the needs of our customers. We
were not the five foolish virgins. We were wise to your gifts.
Your art was oil for our lamps. We were proud to sell "Annie
Lee." You were our stimulus package before bailouts became
popular. We always knew who put America back to work.

She be a national treasure of a sleepy nation.
We who love and know her must tweet, text, email, Facebook,
and gossip her name like she done gone and done something
bad. We must petition her deserved place in America's
conscience. Where is her Presidential Medal of Freedom?
Pre-teen girls learn her story from Grandmother Griots

warning young hands that the faceless statues on mantles and curios are not dolls. Baby girl, that's uh "Annie Lee." That ain't no toy. This one's "Holy Ghost." It's a Limited Edition. Look here; see this big number on the bottom, that mean they only made 5000. Your Mama give this to me back when they was only forty dollars. It ain't no forty dollars no mo'. And Granny ain't got no thousand dollars to buy me another one. That's why I tell y'all, "Don't touch."

Annie, your heart heals; your art heals. You make us proud. You fill an emptiness we didn't know we had.

You are our Picasso, our Salvador Dali.
Keep on healing us. Keep conjuring those spirits.
Keep catching those dreams.
Paint on, my Queen!
Paint on!

Happy-Sad Blues
(Blacklash Blues)

I got them thinking blues
in uh crowd know ah'm uh lone
one moment wants tuh call muh baby
but won't pick up that phone

got them happy-sad blues
feel down but don't feel bad
baby, unnerstand these changes
ain't happy, but ain't feelin sad

heart like uh tin roof
make no music 'til it rain
then thuh whole sky start cryin'
but homeboy, don't feel no pain

make uh rose bloom in winter
make yo' sap cum down strong
like uh mojo in Louisiana
make uh young man do sum wrong

happy-sad blues, they tell me
gots tuh get me uh black cat bone
ever day, hangs it round muh neck
makes muh baby stay at home

gots me uh conquer root
gon' rub in my right hane'
befo ah touches muh woman
so she love no other mane'

keep thuh bed warm, baby
whence n' ever you all alone
cause you know befo' too soon
these blues gon' send me home

happy-sad blues, dey got me
pumped ice water through muh veins
keep yo runway clear fuh lovin'
open yo hangar fuh this plane

put thuh lights on low
keep thuh love nest warm
let thuh tub run fulla water
n' keep thuh love light on

sprankle salt in muh wounds
puts hot water on muh lawn
sprankles goober dust on muh baby
to make her turn me on

Blues, O' Mr. Blues
he dun tol' me whut tuh do
woman if you don't love me right
black snake putta spell on you

now tell me Mr. Blues,
is ah'm right or is ah'm wrong
you puts tombstones in muh eyes
n' makes muh love cum down

dem blues, dey say ah want you
heart say, wanna be alone
but keep uh candle burnin baby
dese blues gon' drive me home

happy-sad blues got me burnin
boil thuh ice water in muh veins
hotter than molten lava
cum on, blow out muh flame

Blues, O' Mr. Blues, ah'm happy
lil' girl feels muh desire
she knows when ah start smokin
cold showers don't stop no fire

half moon through thuh window
curtain shakin from thuh breeze
ah shakes from my woman
when she go down on huh knees

times is hard pretty mama
you got thangs well in hane'
by the way you use your head, girl
ah knows you loves this mane'

take yo time sweet baby
this is vintage "48"
juss sip me like uh highball
n' let the blast-off wait

happy-sad blues done left me
sweet lil' angel blew em' away
muh baby, she never go to church
but she still go down and pray

sun wake me in thuh morning
blues left me in thuh night
ever time muh little angel kneels
ah knows, ever-thang all right

AFTER SANDBURG'S TIME

Tomorrow sits before the fireplace
her thin heavily veined hands lie folded
sleeping soundly upon her frail lap.
An occasional twitch lets us know they are alive.
Her shawl, of muted plaid and autumn, is arranged neatly
about bony shoulders; shoulders that look as if they never
pulled a nine foot long cotton sack loaded with a sharecrop-
per's share. A few wisps of pure white hair escape the quiet of
her matching crocheted cap.
They gather quietly about the nape of her neck,
careful not to disturb her.
".....like corn silk in the wind, torn between competing
zephyrs." She listens to these words, as a slim brown poet ex-
plains the essences of time to a shapely, freckled, long-
legged, red-headed gal from the city. The girl really wants to
believe him.
She dozes, cat-like. Her closed eyelids telegraph REM sleep
signals with Morse code rapidity,
(dash, dot dot. dash dash. dot)................T—I—M—E.
Her hands re-twitch in their sleep.
Much later she rises from her rocking chair.
Gliding gracefully erect and deceptively tall,
she stands on firm, yet, bone thin legs. With a strong lengthy
gait she slips quietly from the place.
The desk clerk raises his good eye from the racing form. He
watches her go. He smiles a glance at his old pocket watch.
He can set it by her movements.
In all the time he has known her,
she has yet to be late.

DEM PEMBROKE, HOPKINS PARK, LEESVILLE, IL.
"CRAZY JOE BLUES"
October 20, 2011

Got me uh patent on yuh Baby
got me uh trademark too
gonna copyright yuh lovin'
and put uh lien on yu

Got me uh order uh protection
uh crooked judge to make it stand
so yu can't get in 50 feet
of any other man

Cause ah want'cha Baby
want'cha all to myself
Ah'm breakin all the mirrors,
so yu can't see nobody else

Cause Ah'm crazy bout'cha Baby
crazy bout'cha, don't'cha know
my friends all call me CJ
you know that stand, fuh "Crazy Joe"

Now yu see why wife
was so quick to let me go
my friends all call me CJ
she call me, "Crazy Joe"

Took uh early retirement
pull'd my 401K
gon' wait on yuh hand and foot
gon' watch'chu night and day

Dun bought up all thuh houses
on both sides uh thuh street
now there won't be no noise
whilst yu gets yo beauty sleep

Yu favor city livin'
me, ah like it in the burbs
now, we ain't got no nayburs
so we cain't be disturb'd

Dun notified thuh post office
tol' thuh cable people too
if you got business wit us
don't call us, we call you

Cause Ah'm crazy bout'cha Baby
crazy bout'cha don't-cha know
Thuh mens all call me CJ
wimmens call me, "Crazy Joe"

Got'cha graveyard plot all paid for
just in case yuh break muh heart
got uh plaque on muh gun rack
say "Till Death Do We Part"

Got me uh lawyer on retainer
got me uh undertaker too
got me uh hit man on speed dial
case somebody mess wit' you

Cause Ah'm crazy bout'cha, Baby
don't want tuh share yuh, wit'cha self
Ah done broke up all the mirrors
so yu can't see nobody else

If yuh ever think-uh-leavin'
Ah put uh bounty on yuh head
100 Grand, if yuh livin'
200, if yuh dead

'Cause Ah'm crazy bout'cha, Baby
Ah want'cha all to myself
Ah done broke up all the mirrors
so yu can't see
nobody else

GOD IS

God is on His throne today
He did not take a rest
He's doing things in His own way
For surely, God knows best

Rain clouds are in the sky someday
We may not see the sun
But we know that in His special way
God knows what we need done

His clouds are invitation
To use our Spiritual mind
To see past all limitation
And discern His Plan divine

And if the clouds somehow remain
"Day-in and day-out"
Our Faith shall rise up and proclaim
"God is God! There is no doubt!"

So listen to Truth's Trumpet sound
As the Saving Grace reveals
All is illusion, we have found
And only God is real

AMEN

DIOS es...

Dios está en su trono hoy
Él no tomó un descanso
Lo hace todo a su manera
Porque seguramente Dios sabe lo mejor

Las nubes de lluvia están en el cielo
Y no podamos ver ningún día el sol
Sino que sabemos que a su modo particular
Dios sabe lo que nosotros necesitamos

Sus nubes son una invitación
A utilizar nuestra mente espiritual
Para ver más allá de toda limitación
Y prever su plan divino

Y si las nubes así se quedan
Por día y por noche
Nuestra fe se levantará para proclamar
¡Dios es Dios! ¡no hay duda!

Así que escucha el sonido de la
trompeta de la verdad
Como revela la gracia de salvación
Todo es ilusión, como hemos visto,
Y solo Dios es realidad

¡AMEN!

Translated from English to Spanish by Tamara LaVille

ALTAR CALL

They partied hardy that weekend
Sin's shoulders were their perch.
Then one said, "let the games begin,
Let's find ourselves a church."
These words a sinner spoke,
The leader of the pack.
To her Jesus was just a joke
Her only Christ was crack.

"Let's check out Casper the Holy Ghost
Somewhere they dance and shout;
The laughs there should be the most!"
She said without a doubt.
A Holy Ghost Meeting Hall
That's where we all should go,
Talking in tongues and all,
Now, that should be a show."

So sure as sin that Sunday,
Puffed up with devilish pride,
They made their mocking way
To a place most sanctified.

They sat up front to taunt and mock
All those who got the spirit.
But it ceased to be a joke
When the leader began to cheer it.

At first her friends did not know
When she began to shout.

They thought that it was all for show
When she jumped and thrashed about.
But when the tears began to flow
One asked her, "What is wrong,
Tell me Miss Thang, I got to know
this an act you putting on?"

Then Pastor said, "There is one
Now delivered from all sin,
Who came today for wicked fun
But found the Christ within.
I want her to come right now,
No need to wait for nerve
And in your spirit genuflect
And say whom you now serve!"
The leader rose up bit-by-bit,
Spiked heels, mini-skirt and all
Ran crying to the altar,
And on her knees did fall,

Speaking tongues of ecstasy,
Crying all the while,
Praising God's Divinity,
Sobbing, "I'm your child."
And if there's another here today
Whose life's come to a stall,
Don't worry, help is on the way,
This is "Your Altar Call."

AMEN

Jesus Is My Role Model

Yeshua is my role model;
I strive for all my days.
He does not coo nor coddle
The sins of Kings or slaves.
He simply made His altar call
Without respect of men.
His message sounded to us all
To repent our sins.
From noble caste to leper clan
This message was relayed:
"Christ as man is in the land;
The ransom has been paid.
Let every hostage of sin
Who seeks God's Holy Grace
And wishes to be born again
Just tell me to my face.
Just stand forth and be blessed
No need to shout "May Day,"
For I've received your S.O.S.
Stand forth and be your faith.
The Christ the Jews thought they slew
Has returned to rescue you.
Did you believe Ol' feeble death
When he lied that I had left?
Did you think I came at random?
Did you think I could abandon
And violate the Ancient Law?
I am the Christ Isaiah saw!
I am God clothed in flesh
Where both earth and heaven mesh,

To demonstrate divine reprieve
To all whom on me believe.
Sure I died, but what's the fuss.
Ol' death could not corrode my trust.
It is illusion, just facade;
Remember children, "I Am God!"
The One-and-Only, that is me,
No Xerox nor facsimile;
No counterfeit nor forgery,
You see God when you see me.
You believe that man went to my moon,
And on your jets you have zoomed;
But when it comes to resurrection,
You are filled with circumspection.
You talk upon your telephones
To loved ones miles away,
And verify through voice and tone
That they are who they say.
And yet, when it comes to me
you want a further proof,
Unasked of the deities
who guaranteed your roof.
You shop and save your receipts,
Your contracts and your warranties,
In event the merchandise
Is less than what was advertised.
My word to you is your receipt
For everything you get from me.
It is a lifetime warranty;
It is eternal guaranty.
I Am My Word..........Try Me."
AMEN

THE ENDING
AND MY NEW
BEGINNING

RAW TEARS

Something come to me, last night while I slept.
Don't-cha know God cried, where it say "Jesus wept?"
I'm crying raw tears, say my pillow's soaking wet.
I calls 'em raw tears, cause they ain't done yet.

I think of the man, fifth Chapter of St. John,
How for "thirty-eight years" he fell for the con.
Waiting to be healed by society's rule,
Never being first to step in the pool.

Jesus cut to the chase, no rigamarole.
He say to the man, "Wilt thou be made whole?"
The Brother start gripping, making small talk;
Jesus say, "Rise, take up thy bed, and walk."

He was crying raw tears; beard's soaking wet.
He calls 'em raw tears, cause He ain't done yet.
He's seeing little Shorties, dying to get a rep.
Don't-cha know God cried, where it say "Jesus wept?"

Her took me on high, and a heaven I saw,
Where reading and writing, ain't against no law.
Between you and me, quiet as kept,
Don't-cha know God cried, where it say "Jesus wept?"

FREEDOM FLIGHT
(RENAISSANCE-3)

(It ain't safe, freedom flight; you gotta leave, this here night)

Little Sonny
talk tuh grandpa
tell meh wheah you been
    dem ol' paddy rolluhs dun bin by
    sez yu ass deep
    n' trubbles agin

Little Sonny
is yu bin drankin
dat gin ah smells on yo bref
    heahs yu bin out
    rollin dem bones
    dun went n' loss
    yo whole check

Duh paddy rolluhs
dun talk wid grandpa
dey sez
yu threaten one life
    n' tried tuh murduh
    Pepper-jo-Boy
    n' uh hi-stakes
    game uh dice

Dey sez
yu shot Pepper-jo-Boy
ovah uh mis-call'd bet

FREEDOM FLIGHT
(CHICAGO RENAISSANCE-3)

Sez he n' thuh County dyin
but he ain't dead yet

Little Sonny
yu gots tuh run
ain't safe
tuh stay heah tuh-night
    dey sez
      yu arm'd n' dain-jus
    dey got orduhs
    tuh shoot on sight

So tek muh seed munny Sonny
set yo' trail
fuh duh Nawf
    keep uh real open eye
    n' uh real shut mouf

Now whin yu gets
tuh Chi-town
look up yo' ol' Aunt Sue
    telluh, telluh
    yu Willie-Boy's Grandson
    ah'm sho'
    she 'membuhs yu

(It ain't safe here tuh-night
yu gotta take that freedom flight)

~ 143 ~

HOME AGAIN

(On being released from Illinois' Death Row,
exonerated after many years of false imprisonment)

If Mary will bake
some sweet breads
if Freddie will come
with his gin

If Ellie will play
my piece on the harp
then I'll know
I'm home again

15 years is a long time, Mary
don't wonder if I'm not the same
15 years of prison sweet Ellie
15 years of change

But if Mary will bake
her sweet breads
if Ole Freddie
will come with his gin

If Ellie will play
my piece on the harp
then I'll know
I'm whole again

MOS: 11 DELTA 10

I am an early riser
years in the military, years alone
and just years in general
have brought this on
with ninja like stealth
I ease from under the light cover
1000 TC Egyptian Cotton
made in India, not China, you said last night
in response to my appreciation of the texture
I am careful not to disturb your rest
you need your 8 hours of sleep you said
as you laid down your two house rules
(those many years ago)
the other being:
"always, always, kiss me goodnight"
I wish you had one of those
memory mattresses, they advertise
the kind that keeps one side from bouncing
while the other sleeper twists & turns
or slips out of bed at 4:30 a.m.
as I do again this morning
I sit on my side of your bed
I watch you sleep
your second pillow wrapped
possessively in your arms
unaware, it is a-soon-to-be-replaced lover
if you get your way
a tear escapes my eye
as it begins to sink in,
you are back in my life............once again

PTSD

Phantom pain pulled at my left chest
heavy-fisted hammer blows struck
where my heart used to beat
where my heart used to be
my left chest imploded
my left arm numbed
I could not smile
my jaw locked; I could not speak
I had nothing to fear, it was not bravery
no need to beat back panic
no urgent calls to 9-1-1
no cries for paramedics, no code blue

I had studied war and its aftermath
I had interviewed and comforted
our wounded soldiers
our brave, frightened,
fighting men and women
our injured warrior kings and queens
aching in limbs surgically removed
by shrapnel, scalpel and saw
reaching now to claw away at pains
concealed beyond the reach of morphine drips
and empathetic eyes
I know the feeling
I know it well
I, too, was wounded

years ago, I lost my heart
and you, and it, are still gone

AUTUMN SUNG
(FROM CHICAGO RENAISSANCE-1)

if you wonder
when you look at me
   what is this change
   coming over me

   don't be alarmed
   there is..........no mystery
   I just change
   like any........autumn tree

you may notice
a bit of orange
   in my walk
   these chilly days

or a burnt yellow tinge
to my casual ways

   and a brown hue
   you may notice
     round the edges
     of my good-byes

   and the red
   you can see

   in my eyes

Inquiring Minds
Want To Know

"What is your nationality?"
said he.

It took me by surprise,
for I was three-times-seven plus
and thought myself most wise.

I had degrees to back my claim,
MBAs and Ph.D.s,

But something in his voice,
froze my answer in my throat
and robbed me of my poise.

'Til alas,
I shrugged in clear defeat,
and asked him, "What is yours?"

He replied,
"I thought you'd never ask,
my friend, we both are Muurs."

DREAMER

when into the arms of sleep so deep
I fall without a care
to play among the many jewels
that I find buried there

should I have known, O long ago
that dreams are meant for fools
who try to lure the gifts of sleep
into their waking worlds

then you awake some morning
to find your dream has flown
and in its place the witch queen reigns
and taunts you from her throne

a thousand and one faceless ghouls
hold court with yester's dream
that vanished like the sweetest breath
upon some frosted pane

yet, you wonder so haplessly
from dreams, to hurts, to dreams
and try to bring it back with you
the lei-of-fantasy, a sleep can bring

Time

Time is a flesh-eating disease
....................airborne and terminal
..............It gnaws at meat and marrow
...........at tooth and tendon
........at hope and dream
at mobility and meaning
....ticking seconds are incisors
.........................ravenous minutes are canine fangs
...............they rip and tear chunk after chunk
of life and memory
....until the thought of you
...........................like a face of Jesus
..................seen in the clouds
.........shape shifts with the wind
then is no more
....gone
....as if you
.............................never were
.......................And even your ghost
..............goes to bed hungry
........and haunts
not a single dream

MY PLAN
(FROM: HOW TO FEEL GOOD
ABOUT YOURSELF)

My plan is worth my weight in gold
with it I must succeed
to reach my heaven here on earth
that I must make for me

My plan is worth my weight in gold
sent forth from God inside
that I might know His glory now
as I in truth abide

My plan is worth my weight in gold
if I just do my worth
I must receive His kingdom come
while I still walk His earth

By the Mercy of the Mother
by the Faith of the Son
by the Power of the Father
It is done   It is done

THINK AB OUT IT

If you want to know what you are planning,
just look at what you're doing.

Do not let your quests in life
be for the consolation prizes.
Be in it to win it!

Do not run parallel to the finish line.

Tardiness has many reasons
but only one remedy,
Punctuality.

Keep your words sweet.
You may have to eat them later today.

When you can believe whatever you say,
you tap into a power, which is only limited by
whatever you say.

A mind is not a terrible thing to waste.
But it is a terrible thing to waste a mind.

There are no success stories
about quitters.

When you think about your loved ones
do you cross your mind?

Life Is A Home-Based Business.

Would you like to live with someone who lied
to you each day? Well, quit lying to yourself.

If it aint "one" blessing, it's another.

While the rising tide may lift all boats,
it does nothing nice for the man overboard.

Too often we work against ourselves,
then forge someone else's signature to the work order,
in order to blame them for our misery.

People often complain about discrimination.
Are you prejudice? Are you left-handed or right-handed?
Have you given your (non-favored) hand equal opportunity in
developing penmanship? Write your name with your left
hand, now with your right hand. Which is more legible? How
long have you had your left hand? How long have you had
your right hand? Do you discriminate against
yourself? Do you give these parts of your own body equal
access to opportunity and growth while you complain about
discrimination from someone else. Have you ever
heard "Charity begins at home?" Try it.

Everyone is self-employed.
It's just that some of us don't know it.

Why don't you mind your own business?

When someone says to you, "You ain't shit,"
why do you become angry and argue with them?

It is easier to criticize you than to correct me.

A Writer Reflects

Sometimes, I am in awe
when I read my words,
not all of them,
and not all the time,
But sometimes,
I wonder if God made a mistake
and meant for someone else
this gift of words
which changed
a shy, sickly Pembroke boy
into a poet.

Sometimes, I have read words
so beautifully arranged,
so tenderly expressed,
that I could not believe I had written them.
More than once, I have interrogated my memory,
demanded that it abandon the journalist's creed
and reveal the sources of its genius, so beyond me.

In momentary lapses of lucidity,
in my flawed and frail humanity,
I have envied the writer part of me who gave birth to
or mid-wifed such telling vulnerability.
Foolishly, at times, I have been jealous of myself.
In all honesty,
I have wondered if my writer's life is a dream,
triggered by some poem or tome
I overheard or inhaled.

Or maybe I have fallen asleep
in my Sophomore year
in the library of St. Anne High School,

soon to be awakened
from a magical slumber,
face down in a book
my place marked by embarrassing drool
and wrinkled pages.

Sometimes,
I fear I will be "Outed" as a fraud,
who hacked Heaven's records,
plagiarized God,
and signed my name to His works.

Sometimes.

ANONYMITY

I should not be able
to read my poem and
pick me out of a crowd
of more than two or three
men and women of various ages.
not even if I sing "I love you
like New Hampshire maple syrup
served with hot-sopping biscuits
made from scratch
by an apron-wearing
over 60 graying grandmother
with nick names like
Gammy, Nana, Big Mama.
No late 30s, early 40 year old
adolescent Granny's biscuits from a box
for my New Hampshire
maple syrup verse"
If I burn my fingerprints off
my pen should conceal my identity
should reveal nothing of me
yet, everything of the poem,
enslaved by quicksand words,
sucked in, snared like souls snatched
from unwilling, superstitious, photo subjects
by arrogant western tourists
with their hi-speed cameras, wide angle lens,
paternal instincts, filters and light settings
My pen should leave me anonymous
unless the ego snitches and sneaks
a self portrait into the line-up.

THAT OTHER MUSE

The connection between the Poet and the Muse
is so special, so tender, so fragile, so sensitive,
so unpredictable, so fraught with contradiction
that one must be careful not to discourage
the approach of a poem whose demeanor may
not agree with your positions and opinions,
on anything,
be it religious, political, racial, social,
sexual, relational, global, etc.

The Muse has a god-like quality
she is no respecter of persons
nor our sacred opinions
the scholar, the statesman,
the highly acclaimed iconic ethnic bard,
if there be one,
cannot expect to pen a finer verse
than the derelict
who routinely pees his pants
as he rides the subway from end to end
reciting stunning lines
he must have memorized from a time
before drink and schizophrenia overcame him

He adlibs life at the behest of his Muse
she is not offended by the stench of urine
nor enticed by expensive colognes

perfectly splashed
on perfectly shaved
perfect faces
In fact, she hates perfection
unless, it is perfectly ridiculous
she does not do prim and proper
she belches, she farts, and around sophisticates
she has been known to pee while standing up
she cannot be embarrassed
her idea of etiquette
is to wipe her mouth with her right sleeve
when eating red meat,
and with her left sleeve when dining on fish

There are millions of these poem-sluts
looking for dates, waiting to be noticed
willing to be knocked up
they live without regret
some are drunken floozies
beautiful, bawdy, loud, obnoxious, desperate
unpretentious, drunken floozies
they will go home with anyone
they will lie with you on silk sheets in palace beds
or on the backs of matchbooks in seedy bars
they will give it up anywhere,
they don't need a room. They don't discriminate
"Eagles don't fit pigeonholes," I heard one say

They will give it up on scraps of paper
or sprawl their wantonness
on finely lined pages of exquisitely bound journals
and for you women Poets,
my Muse has some equally promiscuous brothers
they too will give it up on cocktail napkins
or on congressional stationery
Beware! The Muse. They will give it up anywhere

WORDS

"At the mere thought of you"
words huddle against my tongue
They press hard against my pen
They jostle, they jockey for position
They forego all pretense of decorum
They shove and shriek like unruly kids
Me first! Me first!
Me, Me. Take me!
They crowd together, not like family
but like ravenous stranded strangers
fighting hyperthermia and starvation
after a long arduous trek, weeks without rescue
now, seeking a morsel of warmth
from an unexpected fireplace
They crush against my pen
like guilt-ridden survivors
of a random Act-of-God catastrophe
Now, anxious to call home
to assure equally anxious love ones
on a cold, rainy poem-less night
They beg for love, they cry in their sleep
I pull them close, I hug them
I hug them all at once; I hug them one-by-one
Only then do I begin to write
"At the mere thought of you."

JAN WALDRON

Jan, this is a reprint of something I wrote April, May or June of 2010. I hope I address your question. You asked, "What do I do when my (poetic) inventions are falling flat?" At least, I hope I address it. Well, here goes, subtitles and all.

How I Write

Jan, some poems come through natural birth. Others are ushered in through cesarean section. Some just pop out. Sometimes, I am unaware of the pregnancy as well as the moment of conception. My water breaks, alerting me to the delivery sequence. Ready or not......here it comes. For other poems, we must induce labor and even administer a Grey Goose epidural drip with an occasional cannabis chaser. Whatever it takes to get the job done. *Mea culpa.*

Why I Write?

I write because I cannot afford a psychiatrist. And if I could afford a psychiatrist, I would write because I could not afford a psychiatrist I could trust. I am a closet Catholic. My laptop, pen & paper are the mobile confessional. The completed poem grants absolution.
And I say 7 Hail Yeahs!

Writers' Bloc

I imagine writers' bloc to be a group of writers formed to address a common cause or address a concern, theme or stand in collective resistance to say no to the censorship of malaise or the self-imposed co-opting of the creative imagination.

THE FLOW

As to that other shared misunderstanding
of writers' bloc(k), I decided long ago
if I ever encountered a prolonged period
where I could not write
I would write about not being able to write
I would write of the loneliness
of a pen impotent of poetry
of the hurt of hurrying to a long awaited rendezvous
only to find one's lover missing
or worse yet, present
and presently locked in a sensual sexual embrace
with contemptuous apathy
they grind on one another
they grind fiercely
like unchaperoned kids
making out under the bleachers
after a junior varsity football game
her lover's back is to me
she glares at me over his shoulder
she slowly raises one leg to make it easy
for his unlearned hands to find her
he gropes her in places
I was too cowardly to touch
"She was not that kind of girl," I lamely explained.
"I was always that kind of girl,"
she mocks with exaggerated ecstasy.
she mocks my virginity; mocks my civility.

she laughs, that it was I who was not that kind of boy
beckoning, rebuffing, hot, cold, distant, aloof
she plays the exhibitionist to my milquetoast voyeur
tempting my pathetic lust with a seductive look
showing herself to me, shoving herself close
letting her heat reach me
next, refusing my touch with a withering look
she toys with me, her literary eunuch,
teasing my self-conscious advances
taunting me into uncontrollable angst
fuck writers' block, I grow a pair
I rip her from the arms of self-doubt
I throw hesitation hard to the ground
hard like first orgasms
I take her right there
I take her not like a refined gentleman lover
but a Lady Chatterley-like-liaison
I take her right there in plain sight
She presses hard against my engorged pen
I can hold back no longer.
It's coming.
Coming!
Coming!
I begin to write
I quote her word for word

"I was always that kind of girl," she said.
"I was always that kind of girl."

ABOUT THE POET

I love to write. I have been given a wonderful opportunity. I have a gift. I am not gifted. I am blessed. I am prone-to-poem. As a boy, back in Leesville, Illinois, I dreamed of having a gift. I have believed in gifts for as long as I can remember. I believed Sam Cooke's voice was a gift. I believed that Bob Hayes' speed in the 100 yard dash was a gift. I believed Muhammad Ali's ring prowess was a gift. I believed Chuck Berry, himself, was a gift.

Perhaps, I was being greedy, in wanting a gift, for I've had a gift for as long as I have had memory. I could find anything my family lost, from an earring to the tiny wind-up knob on Grandma Carrie Mae's wristwatch. If it were lost, "Joe" could find it. That gift, however, made the grown folk uneasy. They had no idea how their "human bloodhound" accomplished his feats of mystery. As early as five years of age, I heard the whispers, "Something's not quite right about that child." "That stuff he does just ain't normal."

I had a gift, but I wanted one that would make people like me, not ridicule me. I wanted to pick up the guitar and play and write songs like Chuck Berry. I didn't want to learn to play. I wanted to pick up the guitar and, toute de suite, voilà, I'm jamming like Chuck Berry on *Sweet Little Sixteen*, *Maybelline, Havana Moon*. I wanted to be *Johnny B Goode*. At 19, I received my 2nd gift, the gift of poetry. "I am prone to poem." Stuff just comes to me; I write it down. I dream poems.

Sometimes, I will mishear or misspeak something, and in that I often find the key to a new poem. I sift my mind for leads. I eavesdrop on life. I work in God's secretarial pool. He says, "Who will take a poem?" I answer, "I will." I'm allowed to put my name on it and take credit for it, as long as I don't forget the true Author. By the way, this is my 14th book and I still don't play "Chuck Berry guitar" nor any other guitar. That prize is yet to come. I did get the lyric writing gift. I'm very happy with it, and just like **Raw Tears,** "I ain't done yet." yae & jhm

WHY I STARTED LOSING WEIGHT & QUIT SMOKING TOO

Allow me to set the scene for you. A husband comes home from work. His wife hears the car door slam, looks out to see her man coming up the walkway. His arms are full as usual for a Friday. He's carrying a 12 pack of beer under one arm, a bucket of chicken under the other; flowers and keys are clutched in his right hand. The obligatory cigarette dangles from the left corner of his mouth. She opens the screen for him, but instead of standing aside, she blocks the doorway and says:

> "Make sure you fix the roof
> and finish the basement too,
> in case my next man, Daddy
> ain't a handy man like you."
> I said, "What are you talking about?
> Woman, I don't understand."
> She said, "I know you're leaving me,
> leaving me...for another man."
>
> I said, "Woman, I don't swing that way;
> I don't play for that other side.
> If there were no women left on earth
> I would buy some cyanide."
> She said, "You know I love you;
> you're that apple of my eye,
> and if you loved me half as much
> you wouldn't try so hard to die."

She said, "No matter how I love you,
no matter what I say or do,
I ain't telling no undertaker,
make us a coffin built for two.
You know about your blood pressure
and another half dozen ills,
but you won't change for me nor you
and give your body chance to heal.

You know when you leave here, Daddy
a piece of me leaves too.
But the rest of me will still be here,
still missing and loving you.
Now every time you reach
for that salt and cigarettes,
and your daily six-pack baby,
it fills me with regrets.

You always treat me with respect
that's why I can't understand,
how you could be willing
to leave all this woman
for some other man.
I won't remarry right away,
but honey, you know the score.
I'll miss you madly until I meet
that man you left me for."

THE LEGACY

WE are
　　　our family's
　　　heirlooms

WE are the antiques
WE are the old quaintness
　　　handed down
　　　through generations

WE are our coats-of-arms
WE are our family crests
WE are the rings
　　　　　watches
　　　　　amulets
　　　　　stories
　　　　　lands
　　　　　& legends
　　　　　that have been
　　　　　in the family for years

WE are the prized possessions
WE are the lockets and chains
WE are the antiques
WE are the keepsakes

WE are the recipes of dignity
WE are the heirlooms

WE are the people

THE BINTU AND THE USTUH

Two quarrelsome, yet, industrious tribes lived in a part of the USA known as Northwest Amexem. These were the Bintu and the Ustuh, (pronounced use to). Though their members resided from Canada to Mexico, from the Atlantic to the Pacific, their principle populations were spread throughout Chicago's South Loop, Hyde Park, Beverly, South Shore, Chatham, and Bronzeville communities.

Even though the tribes had been neighbors for more years than either side could remember, they just could not get along. Whenever they would meet, they would have the fiercest arguments. If one didn't know better, you would bet that these heated exchanges would erupt into violence.

According to the Ustuh, the Bintu were forever bragging about places they had been to. They were forever regaling some audience with tales of their travels. To hear them tell it, there seemed to be no place they had not been to. The Bintu favored African cultural attire. The women of the group wore the most beautiful and intricate braid patterns that you could imagine and some that you could not.

The Ustuh, on the other hand, dressed like they were in corporate America. Many of them were. Even the children dressed like they were on their way to a high-level board meeting. According to the Bintu, the Ustuh were forever bragging about all the great things they use to do, use to have, use to be and on and on. To hear them tell it, they use to have, be, and know everything.

Sounds familiar doesn't it? So it's pretty easy to see how the frictions between these two tribes were so easily sustained through the generations. Ironically, both factions descended from four former slaves, Francis, Daniel, Samuel, and Hammond, who purchased their freedom and the freedom of their wives in South Carolina in 1791.

The Bintu were descendants of Francis and Daniel while the Ustuh descended from Samuel and Hammond. The truth was the Bintu and the Ustuh were very much alike. Though they argued profusely, both factions were highly regarded and widely acclaimed throughout the U.S. and abroad. Members of each group were much sought as speakers, lecturers, consultants, and believe it or not, mediators. They were caretakers of voluminous libraries, rare artifacts, first editions and magnificent collections of memorabilia from countries they had been to and positions of prominence they used to administer.

Their first hand knowledge of a wide range of subjects and their impeccable research made them priceless to the community at large. Both tribes were highly educated. A disproportionate number of professionals filled their ranks: Entrepreneurs, CEO's, CFO's, COO's, linguists, poets, novelists, artisans, professors, scientists, attorneys, computer geeks, realtors, stock brokers, investment bankers, philanthropists, and an enviable assortment of successful business men and women.

Both groups were equally respected and praised for their veracity. Perhaps, it was this plethora of multiple similarities which fueled the war of words between the two. For if a Bintu said that he or she had been to Paradise Island, Bahamas to speak during the World Conference of Mayors, a Ustuh would surely reply that he or she used to practically live in Paradise Island or knew someone who used to live there or govern there.

Their "chess match" like conversations moved with the speed and ferocity of a championship fencing tournament and if a Ustuh said that he or she used to study at the Sorbonne, the Bintu would surely relate quite emphatically, how he or she knew someone who had been to l'Universite Paris-Sorbonne, as an esteemed fellow.

This verbal one-up-man-ship, which had fueled good natured, strong, honest debates for more than two hundred years, in recent times had taken on a less than civil combative tone which older and calmer heads found troubling. The young people's verbal animosity reached such ominous proportions that the Elders of the tribes agreed to instruct their respective members to cease talking to each other except for business matters. The Elders set the example. Except for business purposes and the simple civilities of common decency, they ceased to speak to one another.

This decision greatly saddened many of the senior members, but they agreed, without argument, for the greater good of the tribes. Some of the younger men had come close to actual, not verbal fighting, and there had been talk of bloodshed, the type of blood-letting that comes from fists, not guns and knives, but even that was unthinkable and unacceptable, so the tribes ceased talking to each other except when absolutely necessary. This was particularly bothersome to the older people; though they debated vigorously, they knew they learned much from the hard-hitting verbal sparring. It was like the saying, "Iron sharpens iron."

Their exchanges increased their vocabularies, as well as the general and specific knowledge of both tribes. If a Bintu remarked that he had been to the Seychelles and the Ustuh only had a vague knowledge about the islands, you could bet that the next time they met, the Ustuh would sound like a PR firm for that country. It was no secret that both tribes had members who studied from dictionaries to deliberately obfuscate argument and checkmate their foes.

Every now and then some unfortunate outsider would attempt to cross "word-swords" with these walking universities. For their impertinence, they would receive a dressing down from these lexicographers, delivered in such a smooth manner that the linguistic "wannabe" might well come away from the exchange feeling like he or she got the better of the Bintu or the Ustuh. It was often days or weeks before they learned the truth about the verbal exchange and the spanking they had received.

One day, a new tribe came to live among the Bintu and the Ustuh. At first, both Bintu and Ustuh populations were delighted with the prospect of new neighbors. Now, they would have someone else to talk to, to learn from and to educate, but their anticipated happiness was short-lived. This new group, the "Imgonna," were very good listeners but they held no firsthand knowledge about anything of worth. And they lied. Oh, how they lied. And they lied about any and everything, though this was not immediately apparent. They did not lie to get out of trouble or to mislead or for gain, that would have been understandable, and perhaps forgivable, but they lied for no reason.

And oh, were they lazy. They acted as though the world owed them a living. It was soon learned that if you loaned anything to an Imgonna, you may as well kiss it good-bye. That covered everything from a dime to a dollar, from a tack to a nail. They did not know how to return anything but a hello or a goodbye.

What irked the Bintu and the Ustuh the most was a particularly egregious habit which the Imgonna had honed to Samurai sword sharpness. If a Bintu remarked that they had been to Mardi Gras every year for the twenty years preceding Hurricane Katrina, the Imgonna would respond, "Imgonna go to Mardi Gras this year." It would not matter if the conversation were taking place in late September or if a Ustuh revealed that she used to own an organic farm in Pembroke, Illinois, the Imgonna, who had never heard of Pembroke is sure to reply, "Imgonna own me a organic farm in Pembroke, someday."

As stated, not only did the Imgonna lie profusely, they were lazy with a capital "L." It was a running joke among some of the younger Bintu and Ustuh that if you Googled the word trifling, a picture of an Imgonna would pop up. The Elders did not openly condone derisive humor, but inwardly their heads were nodding in agreement. Even when an opportunity arose for the Imgonna to do something they said they were "gonna do someday," they would beg off with one of their standard transparent fictions, and swear that they were "gonna" do it, just not today. No matter what anyone said they used to do or where they had been to, you know the rest. The Imgonna are "gonna" go there or do that, someday.

After a while, the Imgonna had so frustrated the Bintu and the Ustuh, that after months of silence, except for business etiquette, the two tribes began speaking again. It came about this way: One Saturday afternoon, a Bintu car dealer was awaiting the arrival of a team of Imgonna. He had hired them to prep the new cars which were delivered that morning. The Imgonna were over four hours late. The dealership owner was quite perturbed and trying very hard not to become furious. He had promised the contract to the Imgonna before he had learned of their aversion to veracity and there allergic reactions to honest work. With the Bintu and Ustuh, their word was their bond. It was joked about in some circles, that if a Bintu or Ustuh said he or she were going to kill you, you may as well go to the cemetery, find an open grave and climb in. If the cemetery workers question your bizarre behavior, just tell them that a Bintu or Ustuh threatened to kill you. The workers would reply, "Well, in that case we may as well start covering you up." Such was the macabre humor surrounding the unimpeachable reputations for truth of the two tribes.

As the Bintu car dealer paced the sidewalk in front of his dealership, his steps brought him face-to-face with a Ustuh whose auto dealership was immediately adjacent to the Bintu's. Together, they formed the "Auto Mall of America." They handled over twenty makes and countless models of domestic and imported cars, trucks, vans and SUV's. Their combined showrooms stretched the entire city block.

The Ustuh was also pacing in front of his business and scanning the sidewalk in both directions. As their steps brought them face-to-face once more, they glanced at their watches, looked up and down the street again, shook their heads and looked at each other again. Their facial expressions and body language so mirrored the same frustration, that they spoke to one another. Each muttering the same word, simultaneously. "IMGONNA!"

"You must have hired some of those Imgonna too," the Bintu said. "I did," replied the Ustuh . I should have known better." "Me too," the Bintu added. "You can't believe anything those people say. There is no incentive that will get them to keep their word. My Spanish-speaking guys were here when I arrived at 6 a.m. Everyone knows I pay double time for work completed before normal opening hours and time and a half for work done after a standard eight hour day. And they don't try to drag out the work to pad their paychecks; they work so hard, I sometimes feel like I am slacking up on my end." The Ustuh nodded his agreement.

The Ustuh added, "What the young people say about the Imgonna is true." "And what is that?" asked the Bintu. "Do you know how to tell when an Imgonna is lying?" asked the Ustuh. "No," answered the Bintu. "Their lips will move," the Ustuh replied. "Their lips will move?" repeated the Bintu.

At that, the two Elders looked at one another and then began to laugh so hard that tears ran down their cheeks. Every time they thought they were through laughing, they would look at each other and mumble, "Their lips will move." Then another tidal wave of laughter would sweep over them, leaving them leaning on each other, gasping for breath and yukking it up like pre-teen boys out for recess.

The Bintu caught his breath and said, "I've heard some of our young people say that   the Imgonna should change their name to "Ain'tgonna," because they "Ain't gonna" do anything they say." This time, the laughter grew so hysterically loud that the employees of both dealerships came pouring out of the showrooms to see what was wrong. They had never seen Elders behave this way. Even the tribes' legendary arguments never bordered on disturbing the peace like the spectacle unfolding on the sidewalk in full public view. What were they witnessing?

The Bintu and Ustuh workers were so surprised to see their respective bosses hugging each other and laughing so hard their faces were wet with tears and their foreheads soaked in sweat, that they began to question one another about what was going on. The Ustuh knew they did not know, so they asked the Bintu. The Bintu knew they didn't know, so they asked the Ustuh. No one knew anything, except, maybe the two dealership owners, and they were still doubled over in laughter and mumbling incoherently, "Their lips will move," or, "Ain'tgonna," and a new round of laughter would erupt.

So unusual was the scene unfolding on the crowded side-walk that afternoon, that even the Bintu and Ustuh who were driving by, double-parked their vehicles and joined the crowd to see what the commotion was, and why two revered Elders were laughing and crying and acting like they had taken leave of their senses & lost their minds.

On the other hand, everyone was so relieved to find the tribes talking again that the crowd quickly became one humongous love fest. Everyone was hugging, laughing, apologizing, crying and telling how much they missed each other. Some even contacted friends and family to tell them to hurry down to the Auto Mall of America. "You won't believe what's going on! We are back together again!"

And from that day on, when the Bintu and Ustuh would meet, the Bintu seldom, if ever spoke of where they had been to. Likewise, the Ustuh seldom, if ever, spoke of what they used to do. Now, they talked about how much they valued their unique histories and how much they missed each other during "The Silence," as the non-speaking days were called. They would also reminisce and laugh about the mysterious chain of events which brought them back together. Soon, no one talked to the "Ain'tgonna" and eventually they moved away without even saying, "Imgonna go now."

So genuine was the reconciliation that the Bintu would often invite the Ustuh to come and speak of some of their wonderful "Use To" experiences and just as frequently, the Ustuh would invite the Bintu to give a talk on some of the wonderful places they had "Been To." And from that remarkable day onward, there was genuine peace, and un-paralleled cooperation, admiration and love between the tribes. And believe it or not, all thanks to the "IMGONNA."

Thank you for reading this letter & for joining
"The Raw Tears Tour"

Poetically Yours,
Yusuf and Joe

P.S. By the way, today I saw the sinful summer wind making love to a south-side vestal virgin. She was standing at a bus stop with hers or someone else's two kids. It shamelessly lifted her dress, exposed her naturally tanned legs up to her lace panties. It held her dress aloft. It caressed her perfect thighs in plain sight of everyone, kids included. No one lifted a finger to do anything. Embarrassed for her, some pretended not to see. Others eye-raped her. As for me, I confess. I openly stared at this wondrous, all-too-fleeting Act-of-God. It breezed its cool fingers through her hair, enveloped her totally with its touch, bringing an "adults only" tautness to her rebellious nipples, no longer docile, no longer hidden beneath her pale, yellow, silk camisole. It boldly searched her from head to toe, ravished all her secret public and pubic places. She resisted for a moment, released the children's hands. She shouted, "No, No!" as if her words would somehow deter it, as she angrily fought the wind's unwanted advances. She resisted a moment longer, then seemed resigned to her fate, and only appeared annoyed at the over-crowded bus that passed without stopping, or even slowing down.

Will write again, soon,
Love You,
Yusuf and Joe